Beowulf

EDWIN MORGAN

Beowulf

A Verse Translation into Modern English

CARCANET

This edition first published Great Britain in 2002 by
Carcanet Press Limited
4th Floor, Conavon Court
12–16 Blackfriars Street
Manchester M3 5BQ

First published in Great Britain by the Hand and Flower Press,
Aldington, Kent, 1952

A CIP catalogue record for this book
is available from the British Library

ISBN 1 85754 588 5

The publisher acknowledges financial assistance
from the Arts Council of England

Set in Monotype Ehrhardt by XL Publishing Services, Tiverton
Printed and bound in England by SRP Ltd, Exeter

CONTENTS

PREFACE

This translation of *Beowulf* was made in the last years of the 1940s and was published in hardback by the Hand and Flower Press (Aldington, Kent) in 1952. The University of California Press republished it in paperback in 1962, and it sold over 50,000 copies before being discontinued in 1999. In the present Carcanet edition, poem and introduction have been kept as they were in 1952, despite temptations to tinker here and there. The translation, which was begun shortly after I came out of the army at the end of the Second World War, was in a sense my unwritten war poem, and I would not want to alter the expression I gave to its themes of conflict and danger, voyaging and displacement, loyalty and loss. *Inter arma musae tacent*, but they are not sleeping.

E.M. (2001)

INTRODUCTION

I. THE TRANSLATOR'S TASK IN *BEOWULF*

Rifling by chance some old book-tumulus
And bringing into light those iron-tempered
Lines of its buried verse – never be careless
With ancient but still formidable weapons!
                                        MAYAKOVSKY.

What literary activity is more purposeful than translation? And yet, what field is more thickly cluttered with the mere monuments of industry – dry, torpid, and unread! And especially in poetry, what translator has not sometimes felt, with Ezra Pound, that 'all translation is a thankless, or is at least most apt to be a thankless and desolate undertaking'? – thankless, because his audience in the first place almost disbelieves in the translation of poetry even as a possibility; desolate, because of the disproportion between his own convictlike labour and the infinitesimal influence on men's minds of the completed product. Nevertheless apologies are not offered for continuing to attempt verse translation. If poetry has no ulterior motives, the translation of it has, and it is the translator's utilitarian zeal that keeps this difficult redoubt from falling entirely into the hands of its two enemies, happy ignorance on one side and long-term esperantism on the other. When the translator unites with this purposefulness something that was pre-existent in his mind, a secret and passionate sympathy with the alien poet – Dryden and Juvenal, FitzGerald and Omar, Pound and Rihaku, Chapman and Homer, Mathers and Bilhana, Douglas and Virgil – then we may have something memorable, some justification of the activity. The final demand to see propagandist ardour and innate poetic sympathy linked with the care of accuracy – and this is a demand which most critics of translation unconsciously make – is never met in practice, and some translators would indeed argue that any such attempts must be self-contradictory and futile. It is only too easy to stress a 'natural' opposition between poet and scholar, since there are plenty of examples to show that it has existed. Keats's famous sonnet on Chapman's Homer will not seem too strange to anyone who takes the trouble to read that translation as poetry; yet Matthew Arnold, examining the latter piecemeal with a scholarly eye, was able with honesty to pronounce it fanciful, extravagant, oblique, and over-sophisticated: 'Keats could not read the original, and therefore could not really judge the translation.' The point is still, however: could Arnold? And that question remains with us after we read Arnold's own specimen translations from Homer; because these have fidelity without vigour, and if Chapman has vigour without fidelity it is not hard to see whose version will be read, and being read is the ultimate test in such a pragmatic art. This antithesis, real though it has often been, must not be allowed to hamstring the zest of the metaphrastical perfectionist. Communication must take place; the nerves must sometimes tingle and the skin flush, as with original poetry, but to bring this about, 'with poesy to open poesy' as Chapman describes it in his preface to the *Iliad*, is it necessary, is it inevitable that the imagination should deal with its given material highhandedly and inaccurately? Is there not here an attitude of mind, an approach, to be cultivated, a backward and elusive faculty to be encouraged: is there not an art or science of translation, still in its crudest stages, to be developed? The present version of *Beowulf*, for what it is worth, is offered as a step in the direction of 'full translation'; that is to say, it aims to interest and at times to excite the reader of poetry without misleading anyone who has no access to the original.

It is just about a hundred years since *Beowulf* translations in modern English verse began to be produced, and in that period more than a dozen such assaults have been made on the poem. It may fairly be said, however, that not one of these has succeeded in establishing itself as a notable presentation, even for its own period, of a great original. *Beowulf* has been unfortunate in having had no Gavin Douglas, no George Chapman, no John Dryden: the only poet to turn his hand to it has been William Morris, and this translation is disastrously bad, being uncouth to the point of weirdness, unfairly inaccurate, and often more obscure than the original (hardly, in fact, a translation at all, since Morris 'worked up' a prose paraphrase passed to him with increasing misgiving by the scholarly A.J. Wyatt). Nothing has been found, therefore, in these *Beowulf* translations to interest either the practising poet or the cultivated reader of poetry, unless his aim is simply to find out what the poem deals with, and that would be more safely and easily got from a prose version. It must be remarked that the translators themselves are only partly responsible for this state of affairs (less responsible in the years up to 1920, more responsible thereafter), since the problems of verse translation are at any period one facet of the huge general problem of verse composition, and when the existing common tradition of writing poetry, especially from the point of view of technique and craftsmanship but also in choice of subject, becomes as enervated and unworkmanlike as it did in this country between the time of Garnett's translation in 1882 and Clark Hall's in 1914, we can hardly be surprised that the *Beowulfs* of the period have an ineffectualness reflecting a wider decline. Nothing, indeed, could be farther from the mood and effect of *Beowulf* than the neomedievalism of Morris and the Pre-Raphaelites, late Victorian romanticism, the aestheticism of the Nineties, or the mild-mannered prettiness and sentiment of the pre-Georgian and Georgian poets of 1900–14. The period was necessarily at a loss, both in diction and in metre, when it attempted to recapture Old English epic poetry, and the most presentable of these early versions, that of Gummere (1909), can only be described as painstaking and close to the text: it has no poetic life, and its archaism would not now be tolerated. There is not the same excuse, however, for translators who have continued to indulge and perpetuate this essentially late-nineteenth-century undisciplined archaistic pseudopoetic style of *Beowulf* translation, after the first world war and the changes in poetry which accompanied that upheaval. The most noticeable fact about the post-1918 versions is that they fail to establish a contact with the poetry of their time, and therefore fail to communicate, except to those who have themselves no contact with the living verse of their time. They show no awareness of such lessons as were available and might have helped: in Imagism with its insistence on care in the choice of individual words, in the general rejection of literariness, decoration, and the obsolete or bankrupt expression, in the new situational and narrative realism which was being experimented with in poets as different as Owen, Rosenberg, Frost, Day Lewis, and Auden.

Consider diction. The general principle of translators seems always to have been: use archaic diction to preserve epic dignity. Even after the twentieth-century rebellion against archaism (of words and of word-order), this tiresome and usually thoughtless (and hence often ludicrous) tone-raising device has continued to be employed in *Beowulf* translation. It gives us in Scott Moncrieff's version[1] such grotesqueries as 'their sarks rattled' and 'I knew him as a little knave'; and almost damns at the outset the translation of Leonard with its hearty opening 'What ho!' The archaizing temptation frequently conquers the author's expressly or implicitly disavowing it, as a few examples of this curiously prevalent wishful-thinking will show.

Archibald Strong's rendering (1925) into 'modern English rhyming verse' tells us in the Introduction that 'wherever a bold or vivid phrase occurs in the original, I have tried to render it as literally as possible, and for this purpose I have occasionally employed archaisms . . .'. It may be that the Anglo-Saxon poet's love of litotes has influenced the choice of this 'occasionally'; the fact remains that there is hardly a line of the translation without some more or less bizarrely uncurrent term, turn of phrase, or word-order, and the use of archaism is *not* confined to the rendering of something 'bold or vivid' in the original.

> – Then Beowulf the bairn of Ecgtheow his tiding thus 'gan tell:
> 'In my youth full many a mellay and foray grim I tholed,
> And of all at this hour I mind me. I was seven winters old
> When the lord of largesse, e'en Hrethel, the monarch of bounty free,
> From my father took me and kept me, and gave me feasting and fee . . .'
>
> (ll. 2425–31.)

In 1940 appeared Charles W. Kennedy's translation, in what he described as 'authentic modern verse'. Would that phrase at that date, if it meant anything at all, cover such words and expressions as: *Lo!, I ween, smote him sore, what time . . ., blithesome band, 'twas a weary while, wretched wight, wove his words in a winsome pattern,*

---

1 Sniped at even when it appeared in 1921:

> . . . another surly Scot – Moncrieff
> Who brings the early Saxon songs to grief,
> Who translates Beowulf, and then (oh epitaph!)
> Has on the cover his own photograph . . .
> (Augustine Rivers, in *Wheels* 1921.)

'neath, o'er, guerdon, oft, sire, no whit, bills and byrnies, when his soul must forth . . .? Such diction is certainly alien to 'modern' verse practice, and what 'authenticity' can there be in the use of terms which were trite and *passé* by 1600? (A very occasional obsolete word, or obsolete meaning of a word, may be used in poetry with striking effect, but that effect is possible only when the surrounding words are not obsolete; you cannot *keep* smelling mignonette.) Even more confident is the claim made by Mary E. Waterhouse in her translation of the poem (1949), that she is providing 'a clear and straightforward version of the poem, free from archaisms, real or spurious, alike of word, phrase, or verse form'. The amount of self-deception underlying this assertion may be judged from the following select list: *Lo!, thou/thee/ye, 'neath, 'gainst, o'er, 'twixt, 'tis/'twas/'twill, no wise, full oft, whoso, hath/doth, venture grim, the twain, suffered sore, had much liefer, erst, royal dame, ere he wrought, cleave unto, fared forth, most like to, do thou make haste, if courage him avail, whoe'er she be, mine own son, lack for aught, wondrous strong, the death feud hath she wreaked, methinks it is not seemly* . . . Methinks it is not; nor is the claim of the poem to be a version in 'Modern English' a true one, whatever the translator's intentions may have been. Some translators, however, have had a more accurate picture in their minds of what they were doing, and in the Introduction of Gavin Bone's version (1945) – hectic, sprawling, incomplete, paraphrastic, but vigorous and conscious – the translator tells us candidly 'There are some archaisms, but I hope the meaning is plain . . . At any rate there are no "eftsoonses" . . .'

Since none of the verse translations to date has been written in anything like twentieth-century English diction, the reader no doubt feels it is time for me to produce the argument on the other side: the case for the long-hallowed ballad-cum-Spenser-cum-Authorized-Version fixative from which *Beowulf* during the last century has been faintly gleaming like a dragonfly under an inch of amber. This is put clearly and definitely by J.R.R. Tolkien in his prefatory remarks to Clark Hall's prose translation (revised, 1950). 'If you wish to translate, not rewrite, *Beowulf,* your language must be literary and traditional . . . because the diction of *Beowulf* was poetical, archaic, artificial (if you will), in the day that the poem was made.' Now it is perfectly true that Anglo-Saxon poetry used words and phrases which were traditionally 'reserved for verse' and which had been supplanted by other synonyms in prose and in common speech; nor is this different from what we find in the heroic poetry of (for example) Virgil and Milton. It is also true that modern dictionaries still include after definitions of many uncolloquial words the quasi-apologetic explanation 'obsolete except literary' or 'archaic and poetic'. But such dictionary descriptions are relics of a rule of English that has been (temporarily at least) suspended. The reaction against 'rhetoric' has been so strong that present-day readers of poetry will not now readily accept as 'poetic' anything that is 'archaic', as 'literary' anything that is 'obsolete'. And here is the crux of the modern translator's problem, which Tolkien does not estimate at its most formidable. There is no use being faithful to the poetic archaisms of the original if the result cannot be couched in terms acceptable to one's poetic co-readers and co-writers. If it is a case of losing an archaism or losing the poetry, the archaism must go. Whatever the tradition of the original poetry may have been, the translator's duty is as much to speak to his own age as it is to represent the voice of a past age: these are, indeed, equal tasks. If the poet of *Beowulf* was, like Virgil, sometimes *amantissimus vetustatis,* there is no fear of the flavour of an antiquity, a weight and a grandeur, and a melancholy of history, being lost in a version that uses current English; for the background cannot be modernized – the social system, the customs, the entertainments, the supernatural beings, the battles and the weapons . . . and in the inescapable bedrock vocabulary of *king, lord,* and *retinue, gold-giving* and *mead-drinking, coat of mail* and *dragon* and *burial-mound,* the twentieth-century reader will find enough that is remote from his own experience without any superadded linguistic crinkum-crankum and mock-epopeanism.

The metrical problem has been as much discussed as that of diction has been neglected. In the main, this problem has been seen as one of carrying over a poetic tradition based on accent or stress and syllabically flexible into a basically syllabic tradition. (The distinction between 'long' and 'short' syllables, important in the old metric, holds little or no aesthetic meaning for the modern reader's ear, and is usually not taken into account; even if experimentally reproduced in modern verse, it adds no pleasure to it; its significance was lost when the Old English inflections were lost.) Solutions of the problem may be distributed into three principal groups: blank verse, rhyming syllabic metres with heroic or semi-heroic associations, and 'imitative' stress-metres with or without the Anglo-Saxon alliterative system.

Of these, blank verse is the least likely to be successful, although at a first glance it might seem to be the obvious choice, and although it has been among the earliest (J.J. Conybeare's specimen extracts, 1816) and the most recent (Mary E. Waterhouse, 1949) metrical mediums employed. The latter translator argues in her Preface that Old English metric is 'too unfamiliar to be acceptable to those who are not students' and that blank verse is a natural alternative, 'taking it as the modern heroic line and therefore the equivalent of the older one'. If this was the case, the translator's task would be light! But unfortunately it is not true. There is no 'modern heroic line' because there is no tradition of modern heroic poetry; and blank verse is no longer a living medium for extended writing. Tennyson, Browning, and Hardy are the last important masters of it. Perhaps *The Ring and the Book* was the death-flurry of this 400-year-old leviathan; certainly there was not much left to be done with blank verse after Browning (not even by Doughty!), and in Browning the seeds of the subsequent disruption of the metre, to be nurtured in our century by his admirer Ezra Pound, are clearly visible. In *The Dynasts* (our most recent 'heroic' poem – 1908) Hardy did not risk a continuous use of blank verse, but interspersed it with prose and with lyric metres. And Robert Bridges, in many ways a conservative and traditional poet, showed that he was sensitive to the needs of the age (even if unsuccessful in this experiment) when in 1929 he produced *The Testament of Beauty* in a non-syllabic loosely 6-stress line, deliberately avoiding what would earlier have been the almost automatic choice of blank verse for a lengthy and serious work. When we come to poets who are more specifically 'modern' than Hardy or Bridges, the breakaway from blank verse is of course complete and unmistakable: in all the most influential poems – of Pound, Yeats, Eliot, Auden – we do not find it. This means that the adoption of blank verse in translation has the effect of a metrical archaizing, and is merely another barrier between reader and original. In addition, it involves even the wariest of translators in verbal stylizations after the manner of its great users – Milton chiefly, but also Shakespeare and Wordsworth – and these are fatal to the pre-syllabic moods and effects of the Anglo-Saxon. When an attempt is made to escape from the existing (Miltonic) heroic associations of blank verse by using it 'straightforwardly', the result tends to be flat, dull, and mechanical, as in the opening lines of the Waterhouse version –

> Lo, of the Spear Danes' might in days of old
> And of the kings of men have we heard tell,
> How princes then their deeds of glory wrought . . .

– which seems to preserve the primitive bump of Surrey's blank verse *Aeneid* of the 1550s. Above all, of course, is the impossibility of satisfactorily transforming a symmetrical 4-stress line into an unsymmetrical 5-stress line. If you attempt to write good blank verse, you must give up the characteristic Anglo-Saxon midline caesura; if you try to keep a caesura (or, more likely, find it hard to avoid!), then your blank verse will rapidly degenerate into a 4-stress metre with ten syllables. The following lines are an example of the obstinate persistence of the Old English verse basis through a blank verse overlay: the flesh here was too thin to hide these strong bones:

> He lives in happiness; ill health and age
> In no wise trouble him and tribulation
> Clouds not his mind, nor hatred anywhere
> Rouses hostility, but all the world
> Bows to his will . . .
>
> (Waterhouse, ll. 1735–9.)

These considerations seem to show blank verse as the most hazardous of mediums for translating *Beowulf*.

Various syllabic metres, with rhyme, have been much used and well defended. The first complete translation, that of Wackerbarth in 1849, was written in a boisterous ballad measure (coupled with a ballad diction) which is so quaintly and wildly unlike the high seriousness of the original that it is almost attractive, like a double parody, first of *Beowulf* and then of the ballad:[1]

---

1 In fairness to Wackerbarth, one must point out some interesting remarks from his Preface which discuss the possibility of non-syllabic metre for *Beowulf* translation. He writes: 'Some may ask why I have not preserved the Anglo-Saxon alliterative Metre. My Reason is that I do not think the Taste of the English People would at present bear it . . . Still, if the literary Bent of this Country should continue for some few Years longer the Course it has of late Years pursued, it will be time to give this Poem to the English People in English alliterative Metre, and I shall be thankful to see it done.'

– 'And ill I ween, though prov'd thy Might
In Onslaught dire and deadly Fight,
'Twill go with thee, if thou this Night
    Dar'st wait for Grendel bold.'

(ll. 525–8)

Lumsden in 1881, and Leonard in 1923, tried to write at one remove
from strophic or ballad verse (with its romantic, lyric, or short-poem
associations) by disguising the 4-line stanzas as rhyming couplets
and thereby creating a long and supposedly 'heroic' line, of seven
iambic feet with floating caesura in Lumsden, and of six iambic feet
with a clear medial caesura (marked by an extra light syllable) in
Leonard. Strong (1925) wrote in 6-stress rhyming couplets with
medial caesura and what he called a 'swinging' (i.e. it hovers between
anapaestic and iambic) metre. And Bone's 1945 version, irregular in
line-length and uncertain in rhythm, used a mainly 'stanzaic' (*abab*)
form of rhyme and assonance.

In these translations rhyme is employed as the modern equivalent
of the old alliteration, to 'shape' the verse structure, and the metre
attempts to assuage modern ears distrustful of an 'alien' stress-
tradition. We read them with facility, confidence, speed: the
couplets jingle, and we flash along. But is this fluency Beowulfian?
Gavin Bone was surely right when he declared in his Introduction
that it was 'necessary to get away from the couplet'; and in his rhyme-
patterns he has avoided the trite, trivial, lighthearted and even
rollicking effect inherent in the methods of Lumsden, Leonard, and
Strong. But if the couplet introduces a false levity, rhyme itself
encourages distortion and is indeed only thinkable in conjunction
with its many hostages – the tag or the cliché, the archaic word, the
inverted order, the expletive: all of which mar these versions. At the
opening of Leonard's translation –

What ho! We've heard the glory   of Spear-Danes, clansmen Kings,
Their deeds of olden story,   how fought the aethelings!

– rhyme-exigency has displaced 'fought' from the position of
strength it should and would have in its natural word-order, nor is
this a good equivalent of the Anglo-Saxon, for the emphasis is less
on the princes than on their fighting prowess (*hu ða æþelingas ellen*

fremedon!). Or another example: In order to find a rhyme for 'passion', Bone at line 1562 has to write (my italics)

It was good and splendid, titans *did it fashion.*

These are precisely the things a modern translation wants to be able to do without. I have suggested that the long line (i.e. longer than our 'standard' iambic pentameter) is inseparable from a certain tripping or skimming or sometimes lolloping effect that displaces the mood of the original by quickening its tempo. The gravity and 'hardness' of *Beowulf,* its wary, reconnoitring, anfractuous, and often quantal or multidimensional progress (what Gavin Douglas might call its 'knychtlik stile' – in chess as in chivalry), are not achieved by regular metre and rhyme, which by aiming at readableness and smoothness tend always to lose the characteristic (and indeed astonishing) rhythmical variety and subtlety of the original. Harshness must be risked, if we are to recapture anything of this great poem's craggy solidity. The lines must be able to contract to terseness, and expand to splendour.

It is to be noted that the most successful defender of the long line and rhyming couplets ('Nibelungen couplets' as he calls those in his own version), William Ellery Leonard, is also one of the defenders of an 8-stress reading of the Anglo-Saxon line, as against the more usual 4-stress reading. Normally we divide the line into two half-lines each having two main stresses, thus:

Hróðgar m´þelode,   hélm Scýldinga.

But the fact that each half-line may contain a large number of (metrically uncounted) lightly-stressed syllables, as in

Hýrde ic þæt he ðone héalsbeah   Hýgde geséalde

has led some theorists (Kaluza, Heusler, Leonard, Pope) to describe the half-line as having four stresses, two main and two secondary. This, however, merely transfers the problem from the apparently over-long half-line to the apparently over-short half-line, since in the scansion of Heusler or Leonard a great many half-lines have to be padded out with hypothetical musical 'rests' originally occupied (before the days of *Beowulf*) by some intimation from the harp that accompanied the reading or chanting of the verse. Obviously there are difficulties, whether we adhere to a 2-beat or to a 4-beat half-line. If we are looking for an underlying pattern which includes a time-factor then we must either hurry dexterously over the light syllables of the long half-lines or else linger rather ponderously and sometimes in silence over the short half-lines; either way, the speaking voice will have to force some sort of accommodation (not indicated by the poet) if symmetry and regularity are felt to be necessary in the structure. In so far as this is felt, it seems to me much more unnatural to say that a half-line like 'Sidra sorga' has four stresses than to say that 'Hyrde ic þæt he ðone healsbeah' has only two, especially since most of the lengthy half-lines are lengthy with unimportant words which would probably involve slurring and elision in Anglo-Saxon speech. It also seems clear to me that from an unbiassed reading of the poem, whether spoken or silent, an unmistakable overall stress-impression emerges, and that this impression is of four beats to the line, not eight, with a predominantly falling or trochaic rhythm. The examples of 8-beat scansion given by Leonard (*Beowulf and the Nibelungen Couplet*, 1918),[1] with their constant stressing of unimportant syllables, are not persuasive. Should the demand for design, however, lay so much emphasis on the time-element? I think the *Beowulf* poet would have been puzzled by it, and I see no reason why the present-day reader should find it hard to eschew what is after all a bludgeoning of the Old English metre in the interests of the regularity of a later verse technique. My reasons for this will be indicated in a moment.

If criticism can be justly made of syllabic and rhyming versions of *Beowulf*, on grounds of their lightness, speed, monotony, and tendency to pad out and make use of worn or empty expressions for the sake of rhyme, the third group, of 'imitative' versions, stands equally under fire from its opponents. Reference has already been made to the grotesqueness of William Morris's translation, which is in a loosely imitative metre:

The business of bales, and the boot come again. (l. 281.)

---

1 *University of Wisconsin Studies in Language and Literature*, No. 2, p. 99 f.

Scott Moncrieff, who was also called to task for his excessive archaism, produced a stricter imitation (or meant to – his practice was not always up to it) in what he described as 'the sort of lines that an Englishman of the Heptarchy would recognize as metrical':

From many meinies their mead-stools tore. (l. 5.)

But Gavin Bone fairly characterized his metric as 'barbarous and strange', and 'he will not budge a quarter of an inch to be intelligible'! The more moderate and scholarly Gummere fared little better: of his translation, using 'a rhythmic movement which fairly represents the old verse' –

For he waxed under welkin, in wealth he throve (l. 8.)

– W.J. Sedgefield wrote[1] that it confused main and secondary stresses, was full of 'impossible' metrical forms, was distorted in vocabulary because of the necessity to alliterate, and 'it seems a pity to devote so much time and labour to what is after all a *pis aller*'! Nor did the more recent imitative attempt of Kennedy escape: reviewing its alliterative measure –

A baleful glare from his eyes was gleaming (l. 726.)

– G.N. Garmonsway declared roundly[2] that 'it is difficult to assess Kennedy's version, when first one has to dislodge the conviction that alliterative verse is no medium to use in re-creating the poem for modern ears'. This is downright enough, and the translations criticized do not in fact give a very close equivalent of the subtlety and flexibility of the Anglo-Saxon rhythms; yet defence of imitative measures has never been lacking. Wackerbarth's remarks written in 1849 have already been quoted. In 1898 we find a most interesting and prophetically confident statement being made by Edward Fulton in an article 'On Translating Anglo-Saxon Poetry':[3] 'What

1 *Englische Studien*, Vol. XLI (1910), p. 402 f.
2 *The Year's Work in English Studies*, Vol. XXI (1940), p. 34.
3 *Publications of the Modern Language Association of America*, Vol. XIII (1898), p. 286 f.

we want,' says Fulton, 'and there seems to be no reason why we should not get it, is an adaptation of the English, irregular, four-accent measure sufficiently like the Anglo-Saxon line to suggest it at once and inevitably, yet not so unlike the English line as to sound strange to the modern ear.' These hopes were certainly premature, and in the quarter-century following Fulton's remarks any attempts at a stress metre were bound to be up against the obstinately syllabic tradition of contemporary verse writing, and in the latter part of that period against the new practice of the Imagists' *vers libre*, differently but equally unsympathetic. But in the twenties and thirties this situation changed. Partly as a reaction against excessive verslibrism, partly as an attempt to combine natural speech-rhythms with a feeling of pattern, partly as an acknowledgement of the delayed-action revolt of Hopkins, and partly from a generally renewed interest in Old and Middle English non-syllabic poetry, verse whose basis was the stress rather than the syllable came increasingly to be experimented with, often involving alliteration and sometimes rhyme. These experiments have continued up to the present time and include (as I shall show) some well-known and highly successful examples of modern verse in every mood from the farcical to the tragical; now therefore constituting for the first time an argument in favour of imitative metre that must be taken seriously: the argument that readers of verse are no longer unfamiliar with the characteristic effects of accentual writing, and no longer demand at the back of their lines 'the faint click of a metronome'.[1]

The trend from syllabic to accentual, already apparent in Hopkins and Bridges, was remarked on by C.S. Lewis in an interesting essay in *Rehabilitations* (1939) on 'The Alliterative Metre', where he said: 'In the general reaction which has set in against the long reign of foreign, syllabic metres in English, it is a little remarkable that few have yet suggested a return to our own ancient system, the alliterative line. Mr Auden, however, has revived some of its stylistic features . . . Alliteration is no more the whole secret of this verse than rhyme is the whole secret of syllabic verse. It has, in addition, a metrical structure, which could stand alone, and which would then be to this system as blank verse is to the syllabic.' Although it is true

1 P.F. Baum, 'The Character of Anglo-Saxon Verse', *Modern Philology*, Vol. XXVIII (1930), p. 143 f.

that anything like a polemical return to the alliterative system had not been contemplated by the poets, the changes in this direction had by that date gone deeper than Lewis suggests.

In 1927 T.S. Eliot's *Sweeney Agonistes* provided a perfect instance of the old 4-beat stress metre adapted to modern needs:

> She says will you ring up on Monday
> She hopes to be all right on Monday
> I say do you mind if I ring off now
> She's got her feet in mustard and water
> I said I'm giving her mustard and water
> All right, Monday you'll phone through.

Much of the early poetry of W.H. Auden, Cecil Day Lewis, and Stephen Spender was written accentually rather than syllabically, and in Auden, the most influential of the group, there existed from the beginning a strong interest in alliterative as well as in accentual effects. Day Lewis in *From Feathers to Iron* (1931) gives an excellent example of these preoccupations, in the poem 'As one who wanders into old workings':

> Not shy of light nor shrinking from shadow
> Like Jesuits in jungle we journey
> Deliberately bearing to brutish tribes
> Christian assurance, arts of agriculture.

Eliot himself continued to make increasing use of stress rhythms, both in his poems and in his plays. As Helen Gardner has pointed out,[1] the 4-beat non-syllabic line has in fact become 'the norm to which the verse constantly returns'. It is seen very clearly in the opening passages of *Burnt Norton* and *Little Gidding*, or in these lines from *The Dry Salvages* –

> And the ragged rock in the restless waters,
> Waves wash over it, fogs conceal it;
> On a halcyon day it is merely a monument,

1   *The Art of T.S. Eliot*, 1949, p. 29.

In navigable weather it is always a seamark
To lay a course by: but in the sombre season
Or the sudden fury, is what it always was.

But it is especially in the dramas that Eliot has seized the opportunities offered by stress metre, and by the 4-beat line in particular, in the modern poet's search for a continuous medium to replace blank verse and all its inevitable Elizabethan associations. Already in *Murder in the Cathedral* (1935) stress rhythms are uppermost, and are used both for ordinary narrative and conversation (frequently 'pointed' by rhyme and alliteration) and for special lyrical effects like the wonderfully evocative:

Fluting in the meadows, viols in the hall,
Laughter and apple-blossom floating on the water,
Singing at nightfall, whispering in chambers,
Fires devouring the winter season,
Eating up the darkness, with wit and wine and wisdom!

In *The Family Reunion* (1939) stress metre is confidently employed, and is noticeable at some of the most important points of the dialogue, as:

It was only reversing the senseless direction
For a momentary rest on the burning wheel
That cloudless night in the mid-Atlantic
When I pushed her over.

And with *The Cocktail Party* (1950) this rhythm establishes itself with the opening lines:

You've missed the point completely, Julia:
There *were* no tigers. *That* was the point.

It remains basic, though used with freedom and subtlety, throughout this play. The language of *The Cocktail Party* is strikingly less highly-coloured than that of the two earlier plays; alliteration and rhyme are hardly in the picture at all; and yet it has solved with considerable success the problem of patterning racy and realistic speech with just sufficient form to make non-prose effects possible when the playwright may want them. This success, and the acceptability of the play on the stage, argue strongly for the investigation and development of the accentual metres.

The playgoer will also find that the tangential and apparently ungirdable ebullience of Christopher Fry is often, and often at his best moments, formal enough in a stress category though seldom in a syllabic. The author's rather disarming statement in his Foreword to *The Lady's Not For Burning* (1949), that 'every man is free to think of the writing as verse, or sliced prose, or as a bastard offspring of the two', has to be placed, for truth's sake, against poetically charged passages in the play which use a very respectable 4-stress line –

> The night-wind passed me, like a sail across
> A blind man's eye. There it is,
> The interminable tumbling of the great grey
> Main of moonlight, washing over
> The little oyster-shell of this month of April:
> Among the raven-quills of the shadows
> And on the white pillows of men asleep:
> The night's a pale pastureland of peace,
> And something condones the world, incorrigibly . . .

– or against the satisfying accentual swing of lines like

> Hammering the door and yelling like a slaughter-house

and:

> I'd as soon kiss the bottom of a Barbary ape.

In poetry itself; since the second world war, we have two outstanding experiments in stress and alliterative metre, both of which are for different reasons highly relevant to any modern poet's task of translating from Old English. W.H. Auden's *The Age of Anxiety*, a 'baroque eclogue' (of about the length of *Beowulf*) on the state of man in a twentieth-century society at war, is written for the most part in an Anglo-Saxon metre with careful alliteration; it uses a very wide vocabulary, and the technical skill involved is virtuosic.

Richard Eberhart's *Brotherhood of Men* also deals with anxiety and the twentieth century, but is a narrative poem of Corregidor and Bataan and the American war in the Pacific, of some 300 lines, in Anglo-Saxon metre but with sporadic and irregular alliteration.

There are instructive differences between the two poems. Technically, *The Age of Anxiety* gives the impression of being streamlined; its lines are shorter, less rough, less willing to risk the overloading of secondary stresses. Its regular alliteration is a part of that streamlining, but it is less functional than that of the Eberhart poem, since its use is automatic and since the alliterative letter is often concealed in the interior of a word (skipping the prefix: as when 'foresees' alliterates with 'slaves', 'pinch' with 'deprived'). The employment of continuous alliteration, in fact, proves as distracting to both poet and reader as that of occasional alliteration is stimulating. The technical strain imposed on the poet is not outrageous in itself, but the effort, in the absence of such a tradition of writing, is an unfamiliar and (one feels) unnecessary handicap which results in a *tour de force*; the position is paralleled by the strain shown in Old English poets when they try to use regular rhyme, technically feasible in Anglo-Saxon but alien to their tradition. It is fair, I think, to say that Auden's technical preoccupations in this poem, brilliant though the result is, have prevented it from achieving the proper fullness of emotional effect. But it must also be pointed out that Eberhart's task was easier and more straightforward, in a relatively short and narrative poem dealing with a physical situation. *Brotherhood of Men* is precisely right in its adaptation of the old alliterative metre to the uses of a modern heroic lay. The line is longer than the Old English line, which is as it should be, in accordance with the changes in the language; alliteration is used side by side with assonances and rhymes and echoes of various kinds, and also with plain lines whose sometimes strongly moving effect comes only from the 'meaning' and the rhythm and from contrast with the alliterative passages (as for example the poem's last line, quoted below); and the appearance of 'heavy' or harshly stressed lines like 'Played opossum to the enemy's piercing examinations (lines impossible in Auden's scheme) is contextually justified – justified because the present-day reader who knows that he is not here reading syllabic verse is willing and able to make whatever accommodation his personal love of regularity requires and still find the driving 4-beat measure.

The following two passages will serve to show something of the different effects of these poems:

He looks natural,
He smiles well, he smells of the future,
Odourless ages, an ordered world
Of planned pleasures and passport-control,
Sentry-go, sedatives, soft drinks and
Managed money, a moral planet
Tamed by terror: his telegram sets
Grey masses moving as the mud dries.
Many have perished; more will.

(*The Age of Anxiety.*)

And yet I know (a knowledge unspeakable)
That we were at our peak when in the depths,
Lived close to life when cuffed by death,
Had visions of brotherhood when we were broken,
Learned compassion beyond the curse of passion,
And never in after years those left to live
Would treat with truth as in those savage times,
And sometimes wish that they had died
As did those many crying in their arms.

(*Brotherhood of Men.*)

From these remarks and examples, the conclusion reasonably emerges that a translation of *Beowulf* for the present period may and perhaps should employ a stress metre and not a syllabic one; and its diction should not be archaic except in the most unavoidable terms of reference. My own version attempts to fulfil these two conditions, and even if it does no more, I hope that it will make future translators hesitate before pitching their tents at Mickle Byrnie and measuring out the steps to Waxing-under-Welkin.

II. THE ART OF THE POEM

Oh! Blessed rage for order, pale Ramon,
The maker's rage to order words of the sea . . .
                                        Wallace Stevens.

Where every translation breaks down to some extent, is in conveying
a close impression of the *art* of the original, and naturally this defi-
ciency can reach serious proportions when the original is consciously
elaborate and subtle, with part of its flavour residing in the pride of
risks taken and difficulties overcome. We smile at French versions
of *Paradise Lost*; Virgil would wince before the crudity of his
Englishings; and who will put into equally coruscant Russian the
whole alliterative cataract of *The Knight in the Panther's Skin*? The
Beowulf poet, though not a devotee of such technical extremism as
we find in the Celtic or Icelandic or Provençal poems, belongs never-
theless to the group that might include Milton, Virgil, and
Rust'haveli: that is to say, he was consciously an artist in an epic
tradition – and not much less skilful as an artist than these writers,
even if the elements of his tradition were a little clumsier and less
flexible. When he 'unlocks his word-hoard', therefore, we see very
little in the way of botched craftsmanship; indeed he can be skilful
to the point of sophistication, in either verbal smithwork or verbal
jewellery. This is the Miltonic 'elaborate song to generations': the
злато слово, the 'golden word' of *The Lay of Igor's Expedition*: not
perhaps 'a poetry abstruse as hedge-laying', but certainly 'a language
serré, quick with Ithuriel's spear',[1] where the poet, like the phoenix
at midday, *wrixleð woðcræfte . . . beorhtan reorde*,[2] 'with his clear voice
follows the winding art of song'.

It must also be remembered, however, that after the manner of
long poems generally, *Beowulf* has its depressions, plains, mesas, and
peaks. The modern translator, therefore, who elaborates and
involves his style on the working level, in order to indicate the
continuous technical interest the poem has for anyone outside the
old alliterative tradition, finds himself rather at a loss when he comes
to the 'great' passages (since the solution of then becoming simpler

1 Hugh MacDiarmid, *The Kind of Poetry I Want.*
2 *The Phoenix*, ll. 127–8.

can only be used sparingly and by a master-hand), and in addition he may be giving the reader an unfairly heightened or 'fancy' impression of the main body of the narrative, which is sometimes quite direct and businesslike. Variety of texture, seldom attained by the existing versions, is precisely what a reader cries out for when he has ventured into the wood of a long translation. Attention, in all epic, will certainly flag, and if the style used is not capable of rousing it up forcefully or by some wile of wit or allusion or figure-of-speech or word-play winkling it out of the retreat it is sure to occupy at the first signs of grandiosity or dullness, the reader will soon lay *Beowulf* aside, while continuing to admire it for duty's sake; and under such conditions of admiration the poem will never properly enter into literary criticism and be valued at its just rate by non-specialists, as every poem must. The *Beowulf* translator, therefore, who should be so very familiar with the work that he is (speaking at least for himself) in no doubt as to its value and as to the distribution and voltage of that value, should be ready and able to indicate in a flux of textures something of the movement of feeling he finds in the original.

The present version attempts to suggest to the reader the interest or importance various passages of the poem were felt by the translator to have. If I say that such passages are more highly wrought, I may be misunderstood, as this hints at a more conscious process than actually occurs. Greater conscious attention, to all possibilities of alliteration, rhythm, assonance, rhyme, and word-echo and word-linkage of various kinds, is certainly directed on the translation at these moments, with the desire not to let down the relative artistic intensity of the original; but I found the giving of such attention an unplanned need: to bring across anything particularly memorable, I was impelled towards the music of language, 'whithersoever the heart', as Puttenham says, 'by impression of the ear shall be most affectionately bent and directed.'

This applies most obviously of course to passages that are vivid because they are onomatopoeic: like lines 320–4, with their realistic ring and clang of armour and stone –

Straet wæs stanfah,   stig wisode
gumum ætgædere.   Guðbyrne scan
heard hondlocen,   hringiren scir
song in searwum,   þa hie to sele furðum
in hyra gryregeatwum   gangan cwomon . . .

– or the picture of the sailing-ship sweeping through the seas from
Denmark to Geatland in lines 1905–10 –

þa waes be mæste   merehrægla sum,
segl sale fæst;   sundwudu þunede;
no þær wegflotan   wind ofer yðum
siðes getwæfde;   saegenga for,
fleat famigheals   forð ofer yðe,
bundenstefna   ofer brimstreamas . . .

– or the fine resounding shout of Beowulf as he calls into the dragon's
cave (lines 2552–3):

stefn in becom
heaðotorht hlynnan   under harne stan.

Sometimes one wants to draw attention, by whatever means can
be found without distortion, to a very brief but striking phrase: as,
in the Finn episode, when the poet ends his account of the great
funeral-fire of the dead warriors with his comment (for both sides),
wæs hira blæd scacen (l. 1124), literally 'their glory was gone' – gone
like the smoke of the pyre, bravery, *flos ac robur,* youth; or when
Wiglaf the eager young warrior goes alone to help the aged Beowulf
in his fight with the dragon, *wod þa þurh þone wælrec* (l. 2661), 'he
went then through the deadly smoke', as if entering some hell in the
proof of fidelity.

It may be a particular atmosphere the translator has to convey, as
in the famous description by Hrothgar of the 'Grendel country'
(lines 1357–76) with its monstrous Patinir-cum-Böcklin desolation
and strangeness; or in lines like 3021–7, descriptive of the chilling
forethought of an early morning encounter, battle, and death:

Forðon sceall gar wesan
monig morgenceald   mundum bewunden,
hæfen on handa,   nalles hearpan sweg
wigend weccean,   ac se wonna hrefn
fus ofer fægum   fela reordian,
earne secgan,   hu him æt æte speow,
þenden he wið wulf   wæl reafode.

A greater elaborateness, a more 'golden' rhetoric, in the original may demand at some points a corresponding art in the translation, where the narrative must sparkle and the direct speech must ring and sing. Beowulf's account of his swimming-match with Breca (lines 529–606) is partly a gay and heroic self-vindication against the taunts of Unferth, partly an outstanding contribution to the entertainment of guests and hosts in Heorot: the Othello-like utterance, 'the formal word precise but not pedantic',[1] combines with the speaker's narrative enthusiasm to produce some of the most attractive pages of the poem. Another virtuoso performance of the poet, less exciting but more profound, is Hrothgar's long and wonderful speech at lines 1687–1784 – meditation, homily, eulogy, reminiscence and *memento-mori*, addressed now to himself, now to Beowulf, and now to the listening retinue – where technique visibly but always unobjectionably reinforces feeling even at its strongest:

Bebeorh þe ðone bealonið,   Beowulf leofa,
secg betsta,   ond þe þaet selre geceos,
ece rædas;   oferhyda ne gym,
mæra cempa!   Nu is þines mægnes blæd
ane hwile;   eft sona bið,
þæt þec adl oððe ecg   eafoþes getwæfeð,
oððe fyres feng,   oððe flodes wylm,
oððe gripe meces,   oððe gares fliht,
oððe atol yldo;   oððe eagena bearhtm
forsiteð ond forsworceð;   semninga bið,
þæt ðec, dryhtguma,   deað oferswyðeð.

(ll. 1758–68.)

The peculiarly Anglo-Saxon quality of pathos or poignance is very notably illustrated in *Beowulf*. Certainly among the most moving passages in the poem must be counted the 'elegy of the last survivor' (lines 2232–70), the father's lament for his son (lines 2444–62), and such shorter examples as Hrothgar's farewell to Beowulf (lines 1870–80), and the reference to the old warrior recalling his youth (lines 2105–14) – this last a strange and embracing

---

1 T.S. Eliot, *Little Gidding*, V.

recession of art and life, Beowulf telling Hygelac at the Geatish court how when he was a guest at the Danish court he heard the aged warrior telling how the songs and poems that were being recited there ('heartbreaking and true') brought back memories of far-off days and other courts where he himself had received the rewards of youth and courage and heard the songs and stories of far-off days and other courts . . .

> – hwilum eft ongan   eldo gebunden,
> gomel guðwiga   gioguðe cwiðan,
> hildestrengo;   hreðer inne weoll,
> þonne he wintrum frod   worn gemunde.
>
>   (ll. 2111–4.)

The father's elegy for a son who has been hanged employs all the *Beowulf* poet's resources for conveying in a short space the utmost sharpness and grimness of feeling and then widening it out imaginatively into numbness and despair as it takes its place in the pattern of everyday life:

> – Gesyhð sorhcearig   on his suna bure
> winsele westne,   windge reste
> reote berofene, –   ridend swefað,
> hæleð in hoðman;   nis þær hearpan sweg,
> gomen in geardum,   swylce ðær iu wæron.
> Gewiteð þonne on sealman,   sorhleoð gæleð
> an æfter anum;   þuhte him eall to rum,
> wongas ond wicstede.
>
>   (ll. 2455–62.)

Excellences of a different sort are: the nightmarish Beowulf-Grendel fight at lines 702–852 (the present-day reader will find an interesting parallel to its barbaric and prickling horror in the Flay-Swelter fight described in Mervyn Peake's *Titus Groan*); the quick eager lyrical anxious words of Queen Wealhtheow to Beowulf at the feast (lines 1215–31), conventionally establishing her social courtesy, but revealing also her admirable characteristics of warmheartedness, candour, and loyalty; or the grave dying speeches of Beowulf to Wiglaf (lines 2724–51, 2792–2808), so movingly compounded of self-vindication as he looks back and concern as he looks forward, of a care for his own name and honour (with Wiglaf as his Horatio, 'to tell my story') and an even deeper care – the child-less, solitary man's care – for the future of his kingless people. Finally one must mention the quiet nobility of the close of the poem (lines 3165–82), which in its restraint, justness, and dignity, leaves the perfect ultimate impression of the hero's significance.

These are some of the challenges *Beowulf* throws out to the avowed translator, who must make whatever attempt he can to collaborate with the greatness of the original when it is great, and to allow it to speak with its varied voices. If the reader can be persuaded at those points that the poem is good, he will more willingly venture into the obscurer and digressionary reaches of it – the worlds of Finn, Ongentheow, and Thryth: and even these, structurally alarming though they may seem, as episodes, analogies, prophecies, and elab-orated narrative interjections of praise or blame, should not for long daunt any reader who thinks of the methods of the contemporary novel, or, for that matter, of the methods of epic and drama in general. Although *Beowulf* is a narrative, its author was no more 'simply telling a story' than Virgil or Milton or Joyce was, and the interruptive and illustrative material is seldom if ever irrelevant to the broader purposes of the poet. Narrative and episodes are equally concerned with the workings of providence (whether 'God' or 'wyrd') and with both the psychology and the morality of human actions. If a distant or even legendary incident seemed to throw light on the character of the hero, whether by contrast or by reinforce-ment, it would be made use of at some point, as the story of Heremod is brought into Hrothgar's 'sermon'. Lyric relief; sentiment; didactic comment; historical vistas; exclamations of surprise and awe; ironies and by-laconisms – all find a part in a poem that has already succeeded in interlocking (with one or two frayed patches) pagan and Christian, local and universal, factual and imaginary. Seriousness, the poet's most obvious characteristic and the unifying and dignifying force behind the diverse material, was clearly not incompatible with sallies into other modes, though pervasive enough to suggest more often than not the playfulness of the bear or the jocu-larity of the hangman.

That seriousness and that unification and that dignity are embodied in the figure of Beowulf, who bestrides the two parts of the poem and can leave only the severest critic with a complaint of its disjointedness which is based on *feeling* as well as on an intellectual awareness of the split at line 2200. If, in Chapman's striking phrase, we can still see Homer's 'naked Ulysses clad in eternal fiction',[1] so too we can see Beowulf. Out of the trappings of the Heroic Age, out of the conventions of a military aristocracy and the transitional refinements of its Christianization, out of the monstrous fictive quasi-satanic evil materialized in Grendel-brood and dragonkind, he starts up as man and as example: naked, he is courage, magnanimity, service to the point of sacrifice, 'not passion's slave'; and yet the fiction too is a dignity and something more than relative and historical, because the poet has been concerned to make a living issue of the good ordering of lord-and-retainer society and has presented its attractiveness as he has presented its tragedy, so that its tangled loyalties and dilemmas are as real to us as the situations in Greek or Elizabethan drama, and Beowulf clad, Beowulf the folk-king, Beowulf as Hrothgar's all-but-son and Wiglaf's all-but-father, makes the gross fictive ambience flash and resound and persist. In that ambience, an adversary like Grendel shares with him the fusion of fiction and truth: on the one hand Grendel is a superstitious embodiment of danger among peoples whose struggling civilization and amenity are only a stockade in a hostile or unexplored environment, on the other hand he is a lasting figure of the diabolical, anti-human and anti-divine; as he prowls in misery and hatred round the lighted clamorous festivity of Heorot hall, 'the outcast spirit haunting darkness', he is Iago at Cyprus, Satan in Milton's Eden with his 'sight hateful, sight tormenting!', Claggart watching Billy Budd, Quint turning the screw in the soul of Miles. If the poem was only a record of sixth-century Scandinavian calamities, deliverances, and forebodings; or if it was only a palimpsest of distorted and rebarbative mythology: we could still speculate well on its historical curiosity, as we do with the whetstone of Sutton Hoo. It is, however, something more than an object of speculation. Its narrative is the story of a dedicated hero whom we rejoice to sympathize with as heroic; its battles are battles of good and evil; its moral commentary is an unsupplantable lyricism: *swylc sceolde secg wesan*, 'if all men

---

1 Epistle Dedicatory to his translation of the *Odyssey*.

were like him – !' Heroic narrative? Battle-poetry? Moral commentary? Perhaps these strange terms are to our times either wraiths or bugaboos or both. Let those who shy at them read *Beowulf* – for something serious which is kept alive by a deep fantasy, for something traditional, strong, and severe, which must return.

EDWIN MORGAN

NOTE ON TEXT

The translation is based on the text of Klaeber's third edition (revised), but other editions have been consulted and Klaeber's reading has not always been followed.

Passages in square brackets, marked with an asterisk, represent either presumed omissions in the Beowulf manuscript or parts of it which are too badly damaged to be read with any certainty.

E.M.

BEOWULF

How that glory remains in remembrance,
Of the Danes and their kings in days gone,
The acts and valour of princes of their blood!
    Scyld Scefing: how often he thrust from their feast-halls
The troops of his enemies, tribe after tribe,
Terrifying their warriors: he who had been found
Long since as a waif and awaited his desert
While he grew up and throve in honour among men
Till all the nations neighbouring about him
Sent as his subjects over the whale-fields   10
Their gifts of tribute: king worth the name!
Then there was born a son to succeed him,
A boy for that house, given by God
As a comfort to the folk for all the wretchedness
He saw they had lived in, from year to year
Lacking an overlord; and the overlord of Life,
Of Glory, gave the man worldly excelling,
Till his fame spread far, the fame of Beowulf
The son of Scyld, on Scandinavian soil.
So should magnanimity be the young man's care,   20
Rich gifts and royal in his father's household,
That when he is old his ready companions
Will remain with him still, his people stand by him
When war returns; a man shall flourish
By acts of merit in every land.
    Then Scyld departed in the ripeness of time,
Old in deeds, to the Lord's keeping.
They carried him down to the restless sea,
His beloved retainers, as he himself had asked
While words served him, the lord of the Scyldings   30
And their dear king who had ruled them long.
There at the harbour stood the ring-prowed boat,
The prince's vessel, ice-cased, sea-keen;
Deep in the ship they laid him down,

1

Their beloved lord, the giver of rings,
The hero by the mast. Great treasures there,
Far-gathered trappings were taken and set:
No ship in fame more fittingly furnished
With weapons of war and battle-armour,
With mail-coat and sword; there lay to his hand   40
Precious things innumerable that would go at his side
Voyaging to the distant holds of the flood.
By no means poorer were their rich offerings,
The treasures they gave him, than those given
By the men who cast him at his life's beginning
A child out over the waves alone.
Lastly they put up high above his head
A gold-woven banner, and let the sea bear him,
Gave him to the main; their hearts grieved,
Mourning was in their minds. And whose were the shores –   50
Who can say with truth, whether counsellor in hall
Or warrior on earth – where this freight was washed?
    That country then saw Beowulf of the Scyldings
Renowned among the peoples, a beloved king
Ruling many years – his father and lord
Having gone from the world – until there was born to him
Noble Healfdene; war-grim, aged,
Lifelong guardian of the illustrious Scyldings.
By him four children reckoned in all
Were born into this world, princes of men,   60
Heorogar and Hrothgar and the good Halga
And she *[. . . . . .], who was Onela's queen,
The dear consort of the warlike Swede.
To Hrothgar in time came triumph in battle,
The glory of the sword, and his friendly kinsmen
Flocked to serve him till the band of them was great,
A host of eager retainers. And his mind
Stirred him to command a hall to be built,
A huger mead-house to be made and raised
Than any ever known to the children of men,   70
Where he under its roof to young and old
Would distribute such gifts as God gave him,
Everything but the lands and lives of his people.

Not few, we are told, were the tribes who then
Were summoned to the work far throughout this world,
To adorn that dwelling-place. And so in due time,
Quickly as men laboured, it was all prepared,
Most massive of halls; and he called it Heorot
Whose word was authority far and wide.
And his promise he performed, he presented rings,   80
Treasure at banqueting. The hall towered up
Clifflike, broad-gabled: (it awaited flame-battling,
Fire's hostility; and not far off
Lay that sword-hatred ready to be roused
In the deadly feud of father and son-in-law).
   But the outcast spirit haunting darkness
Began to suffer bitter sorrow
When day after day he heard the happiness
Of the hall resounding: the harp ringing,
Sweet minstrelsinging – as the tongue skilled   90
In the distant conception and creation of men
Sang how the Almighty made the earth-fields
Brilliant in beauty, bound by the sea,
Set exulting sun and moon
As lamps for the light of living men,
And loaded the acres of the world with jewelwork
Of branch and leaf, bringing then to life
Each kind of creature that moves and breathes.
– So those retainers lived on in joy
Happy all, till this one spirit,   100
Hell in his mind, his malice began.
Grendel the fiend's name: grim, infamous,
Wasteland-stalker, master of the moors
And the fen-fortress; the world of demonkind
Was for long the home of the unhappy creature
After his Creator had cast him out
With the kin of Cain, the everlasting Lord
Destining for the death of Abel killed;
A joyless feud, for he banished him far,
His Maker for his crime, far from mankind.   110
Progenitor he was of the miscreations,
Kobolds and gogmagogs, lemurs and zombies

3

And the brood of titans that battled with God
Ages long; for which he rewarded them.
　He went then to visit at the fall of night
That lofty hall, to see how the Danes
Fared as they lay at the end of their carousing.
Within it he found the band of warriors
Sleeping after the feast; they were far from sorrow
And the misery of men. The creature was like pestilence 　120
Raging and ravenous, quick at his task,
Savage and unsparing, seizing thirty
Soldiers from their beds; then off again
Glutlusty with booty making for his home,
Seeking his dwelling laden with the slain.
When the dawn broke and day began
And Grendel's battle-strength filled men's eyes,
Then weeping arose where feasting had been,
Loud morning crying. The illustrious king,
The man old in worth sat unrejoicing, 　130
Bearing, enduring grief, strong
Sorrow for his soldiers, when they saw the footprint
Of the hated, of the accursed spirit; that strife
Was too strong, too long, and too malignant!
And after no longer than a single night
He went further in murder and mourned none for it,
In hatred, in violence – in these ways too set.
Then it wasn't rare for a man elsewhere
At a greater distance to look for his rest,
For a bed in the outbuildings, when once he knew, 　140
Truly told by a sure token,
The hall-haunter's hate; to escape the fiend
Was to keep himself thereafter farther off and safer.
So he held sway and struggled against the right,
Solitary against all, till empty and unvisited
Stood the best of halls. Long was the time,
Twelve years passing, that the lord of the Scyldings
Spent to learn pain, each grief there was,
Each bursting sorrow; and so it became known,
Became open to men, grievously recounted 　150
To the children of men, how Grendel fought

That time with Hrothgar, waging his enmity,
His sin-forced feud for many seasons,
His seasonless strife; what peace would he have
With any man of the host of Denmark?
His deadliness was unshakeable: no settling with money:
Nor did any counsellor have cause to expect
Glorious reparation from the killer's hands;
But that was a monster remorseless to persecute,
Dark with death's shadow, both veteran and untried;   160
He lay hid and plotted, he held the moors,
Mist, endless night; and what man's knowledge
Can map the gliding-ground of demon and damned?
   So mankind's enemy, the terrible solitary
Went on accomplishing outrage on outrage,
Heavy humiliations. Heorot was his house,
That treasure-strewn hall through the hours of blackness.
(– No coming openly to the throne or its gifts
Or feeling its favour, forbidden by God.)
It was sharp distress to the lord of the Scyldings,   170
Heartbreak it was; often his chief men
Gathered in council to debate the means
That might seem best to the brave in mind
For combating the panic terror of the raids.
At times in their temples they made pagans' vows,
Sacrifices to their idols, in their speeches beseeching
The destroyer of souls to help the people
In their common affliction. Such was their custom,
The hope of the heathen; it was hell that came
Called back to their minds, of the Creator they knew nothing, 180
The Judge of all acts, the Lord God was strange to them,
And indeed they were ignorant of the praise of heaven's King,
The Ruler of Glory. O unhappy man
Who will thrust his soul through terrible perversity
Into Fire's embrace, eschewing solace
All unregenerate! O happy the man
To be drawn to the Lord when his death-day falls,
In his Father's embrace to implore his peace!
– So the son of Healfdene's heart was surging
With the cares of that time, nor could the wise man   190

Turn aside his trouble; the strife too severe,
Too long, too malignant, that settled on that people,
Fierce-forcing persecution, night-frightfulness unequalled.

[194–1250] *Beowulf and Grendel*

This Grendel feud became known at home
To Hygelac's warrior, brave among the Geats:
Who at that hour of this earthly life
Was master of manhood of all mankind,
Great-framed, greatheart. He had himself prepared
A sound sea-vessel, and said he would visit
The strong king beyond the swan's-way,   200
The illustrious prince desperate for men.
From that expedition he was little dissuaded
By friends and advisers, though to them he was dear;
They urged the hero on, they augured him well.
The good man had picked out from the people of the Geats
Soldiers who were the eagerest among those he could find,
And with a band of fourteen men collected
He made for the boat, the warrior led the way,
The sea-skilled man to the fringe of the beach.
Not long after was the vessel on the waves,   210
The boat beneath the cliff. The men, alert,
Leapt onto the prow; surf was swirling,
Sand was stirring; soldiers took up
Into the ship-hold glittering trappings,
Splendid battle-arms; and the men cast off,
Eager voyagers, in their tight-timbered boat.
Off over the choppy sea, wind-whipped,
The foam-throated thing went bobbing like a bird,
Till after a space on the second day
The winding prow of the ship had advanced   220
To where the seafarers had glimpse of land,
Could see cliffs gleaming, sheer fall of bluffs,
Ample promontories: they had crossed the sea,
Their voyage was ended. They quickly then
Climbed onto the shore, the men of the Weders,

And moored the ship; mail-coats clashed,
Trappings of battle. They gave thanks to God
For the grace he had shown in their safe seagoing.
  But the Scyldings' coastguard gazing from his rock,
He whose duty was to watch the sea-cliffs,   230
Saw shining shields borne across the gangplank,
Saw bared battle-gear; and his thoughts were pricked
With desire to discover the strangers' business.
So he came to the shore, mounted on horseback,
Hrothgar's man, brandishing with force
A formidable spear, and uttered these words:
'What men would you be, here in your armour,
Mail-coat-protected, in that tall ship
Brought through the paths and acres of ocean
Here, to our land? Long have I been   240
A watcher on these coasts, my vigil the sea,
Lest any enemy with warship-convoy
Should come to plunder the country of the Danes.
Never more openly have shield-armed men
Made harbour here, yet where is your permission,
Pass of any kind from our commanders,
Consent from the court? I never looked on
A finer man living than one of you seems,
He there in his armour: no mere retainer
Tricked out with weapons, unless looks belie him,   250
Looks without equal. Now I must know
Who you are, and from where, in case from this point
You push forward into Denmark and are taken as spies
As you move on inland. So now far-sailers
From homes sea-hidden, bend your attentiveness
To my plain request: promptly to tell me
Where you have come from, in courtesy is best.'
  The leader it was who gave him reply,
The commander of the company, from his word-treasury:
'We are men belonging to the nation of the Geats,   260
We are hearth-companions of Hygelac.
Well-known was my father among the peoples,
A princely battle-chief, Ecgtheow his name;
Many many years he lived before he left us,

7

Went old from our courts; him every counsellor
Happily remembers far and wide.
With friendly purpose we have come to seek
Your own overlord, the son of Healfdene,
Protector of his people; give us fair forwarding!
To that renowned man, ruler of the Danes,   270
We have a great mission; and this not, I may say,
Secret in any way. You know (if indeed
Things have run as rumour has reached us)
How among the Scyldings a certain persecutor,
A mysterious destroying-force in the deep of night,
Unveils to dread a malignity unfathomable,
Murderousness, humiliation. I might in magnanimity
Give Hrothgar advising for the remedy of that,
How he, old and trusted, could overcome this fiend
(If ever again he is to find a reversal,   280
A cure for the care of slaughter and evil),
And affliction's flames become assuaged –
Or else he may suffer ever after
Distress and oppression as long as there stands
On that thronelike site his hall of halls.'
    The officer spoke, seated on his horse,
The guard unfearing: 'Keen shield-fighter
Of any circumspection must know how to judge
And distinguish the worth of both words and deeds.
You are, as I have heard, a troop loyal   290
To the lord of the Danes; go forward now
With your arms and armour, and I shall be your guide.
Also I shall have my men hold fast
In safe keeping against any enemy
Your buoyant boat, your ship on the sand
Fresh from its tarring, till it carries again
Its beloved man through the winding tides,
The winding prow to the land of the Weders,
With such of the generous and brave as it is given
To survive in safety the storm of battle.'   300
    Then they set off: the boat lay at rest,
The broadbreasted ship rode on its mooring,
Its anchor was fixed. Each helmet sparkled

With its glancing boar-emblems: brilliant with gold,
Patterned and fire-tempered, it guarded the life
Of its brave battle-wearer. The men hastened,
They marched together until they could see
A timbered building resplendent with gold:
The most illustrious hall under heaven
For men to move in, and home of a king: 310
Like a lantern illuminating many lands.
Here the soldier showed them the dazzling
Hall of the heroes, pointed the approach
Their steps were to take; and with this the warrior
Wheeled round his horse, and sent back speech:
'Now I must leave you; may the omnipotent
Father hold you in the favour of his keeping,
Your ventures be blessed! I shall be at the shore
To hold watch and ward for war-bent host.'
The street was paved with stone, the men   320
Followed on together. War-chains shone,
Strong-linked, hand-locked, glittering ring-mail
Gave iron song-of-arms as they first approached
Marching on to the hall terrible in their battle-trappings.
Their broad shields they laid, the weary seafarers,
Hardest of bucklers at the wall of the building,
And sat at the bench. – The armour rang,
The war-gear of those men; the spears were stacked
Standing all together, weapons of the voyagers,
Ash-cut, grey-tipped; appointed for all fighting   330
That mail-clad band! A nobleman there
Inquired of the warriors their house and kindred:
'Where is it you come from with your gold-laden shields,
Your grey mail-coats and your masked helmets,
Your store of spears? I am Hrothgar's
Personal messenger. Never did I see
Strangers of your number finer than you seem.
The love of arms, I should say, not exile,
Mind's magnanimity brought you to Hrothgar?'
Duly he answered him then dauntless,   340
Hero of the Weders, spoke up in answer
Strong in his armour: 'We are Hygelac's

9

Table-companions; my name, Beowulf.
Let me declare to the son of Healfdene,
To the illustrious prince what my mission is,
Tell it to your king, if he will permit us
To stand before him worthiest of men.'
Wulfgar spoke, a man of the Wendels,
Well-known to many in mind and character
For wisdom and valour: 'That I shall ask   350
The lord of the Danes, protector of the Scyldings,
Giver of rings, as you make petition,
Ask the great prince concerning your visit,
And quickly report to you what reply
The king in his goodness thinks fit to give me.'
He turned then at once to where Hrothgar sat
Aged and grey in the midst of his retinue;
The warrior went and stood facing
The ruler of the Danes in rite of decorum;
Wulfgar spoke to his protector and lord: 360
'Here have arrived, come from far off
Over miles of the sea-flood people of the Geats;
Beowulf is the name these soldiers give
To the man who leads them. They come to ask
That they might, my lord, exchange at this time
Speech with yourself; you should not refuse them
A reply in this, gracious Hrothgar –
For they seem in their armour to be very candidates
For the esteem of kings, and certainly their commander
Who led the men here commands by right!'   370
Hrothgar spoke, defender of the Scyldings:
'Him I knew when he was but a boy;
His father was old, Ecgtheow he was called,
And Hrethel of the Geats gave him in marriage
His only daughter; his son now has come
Here in his strength to a tested friend.
What did seafarers, taking gifts to the Geats
For their pleasure yonder, say of the man –
That he holds in the grip of his hands the strength
Of thirty others, a hero blazoned   380
In valour's report? It is in the favour

Of holy God that he comes to visit us,
Comes to the Danes, comes (as I believe)
For the horror of Grendel. To him in his excellence,
For his fiery purpose, I shall tender treasures.
Now no delay, but invite him in
To the company of my retinue gathered together;
And tell him also that his men are welcome
To this Danish folk.' *[Wulfgar went then
To the door of the hall] and called from within: 390
'My master, the victorious king of the Danes,
Has ordered me to tell you that he knows your kinsmen,
And that you who have come in your determination
Here over the sea-swell are welcome to him.
Now you may go in your battle-trappings,
War-mask-helmeted, to see Hrothgar.
Let these fighting-spears of yours stay here,
Death-wood, death-shafts, till you have spoken together.'
    Then the ruler rose surrounded by his soldiers,
Thick-thronging retinue; some remained there   400
To guard the battle-gear as the brave man required them.
They hastened in a group, the warrior leading,
Under Heorot's roof; the hero went in,
Helmeted, grave, till he stood at the hearth;
Beowulf spoke (his war-net shone on him,
Magically chained by skills of smithcraft):
'Your life and health, Hrothgar! I am Hygelac's
Kinsman and retainer; many a hard venture
Has my youth endeavoured. Word about Grendel
Came to me clearly on my native soil: 410
Sea-travellers tell that this hall stands
(Building of buildings for every warrior)
Void and unused when the light of evening
Has been hidden under the hood of heaven.
And then my people, the best of men,
Deliberating well, began to advise me,
My lord Hrothgar, to seek you out,
For they were aware of the force of my strength:
Themselves looked on as I came from battle,
Bloodied from my enemies, where I took five captive,   420

11

Ravaged giantkind, and on the waves by night
Slaughtered the krakens, suffered sharp stress,
Crushed them in their fierceness, avenged Geats' grief –
They courted their hurts! – ; and now I am here
For this fiend, for Grendel, to settle with these hands
The demon's account. Prince of the Danes,
I have now therefore to make you this request,
This single petition, protector of the Scyldings,
Not to forbid me, defender of fightingmen,
Folk-friend endeared, far as I have come,   430
To try with these hands and my company of men,
This unswerving troop, to sweep Heorot clean.
I have found out also that this is a monster
Recklessly bold in refusal of weapons:
So let me despise – and then may Hygelac
Have me his liege in his thoughts with pleasure –
The military assumptions, yellow shield, sword,
Broad-rimmed buckler, and let me rather
Grapple with the fiend in mortal wrestlehold,
Hated against hateful; with submission in him   440
To the will of God who is taken by death.
I am sure that he if he has the power
Will feast unfearing in the warriors' hall
On the Geatish folk as he often has done
On the host of the Danes. Never will you need
Turf for this head, if death takes me,
For I shall be with him crimson-sullied:
He carries off his blood-plunder, its taste is in his mind,
The outcast feeds far from sorrowfully,
Threads the waste dales; you will never be burdened   450
With an hour's anxiety for my body's keeping.
Send off to Hygelac, if battle takes me,
That best of war-coats and my breast's defence,
Most excellent of armour; it is Hrethel's heirloom
And work of Wayland. Fate must be fate!'
   Hrothgar spoke, protector of the Scyldings:
'In the memory of deeds done, in the service of honour
You have come to visit us, Beowulf my friend.
Your father instigated the greatest of feuds;

Heatholaf he killed with his own hands   460
Among the Wylfings; and then the Weder-folk
Didn't dare hold him for fear of invasion.
From there he went to the people of the Danes,
Over the wave-swell to Scylding soil.
I had just succeeded to the Danish throne,
Holding in my youth this far-spread kingdom
With its walled magnificence and its living souls;
Heorogar was dead, dead my brother,
Child of Healfdene, my elder – and my better.
Afterwards I settled that feud with reparations,   470
I sent the Wylfings across the sea-crest
Old precious gifts; and he swore me his oaths.
Misery it is for my mind to be telling
Any living man what Grendel has done
To humiliate me in Heorot by devices of his hate,
What terror-raids made; my hall-warrior-band,
My battle-troop is thinned: doom-swept away
To Grendel and horror. How easily God
Might cut off the blind destroyer from his acts!
Warrior after warrior, in the flush of drinking,   480
Has been loud with his boasts above the ale-cup
To be in the beer-hall lying in wait
With daunting blade for Grendel's assault.
– But see this mead-house when morning came,
The rich hall blood-red in the light of day,
The entire bench-space drenched with crimson,
The palace with battle-blood; and my friends the fewer,
My beloved chivalry, for death's theft there.
– Sit now at the banquet, and unbind your thought
To the people of the Danes as your mind may urge you.'   490
    Then for the Geats who were gathered together
A bench was cleared within the beer-hall,
Where the warriors went to take their seats
In the joy of the pride of life. An attendant
Was serving, took round the sumptuous ale-flagon,
Poured gleaming mead. Heorot would ring then
To the clear-voiced minstrel. There men had joy,
Danes' joy and Weders' joy, in no puny retinue.

Unferth spoke, the son of Ecglaf,
Sitting at the feet of the Scylding king,   500
Let out some malice – the coming of Beowulf,
Seafarer and hero, having powerfully riled him
For his own unwillingness to have another man,
Any under the sun, ever attain
More glory on earth than he himself – :
'Are you that Beowulf who challenged Breca
In a proof of swimming-strength on the great sea
When the two of you out of vainglory made trial of the waters
And for a foolish vow ventured your lives
On the skin of the abyss? The man was lacking,   510
Either friend or enemy, who could turn you back
From the hazardous undertaking as you swam from the shore.
There with your arms you embraced the tide,
Traced out the surging miles and with flailing
Palms thrust flashing through the waves; the swell
Was bridling up with its wintry seethings.
Seven nights' labouring on in the brinehold,
And he outswam you, he had the mastery.
The dawn-flood threw him on a Norway beach.
Dear to his folk, he left there to seek   520
His native soil, the land of the Brondings,
The pleasant fortress where he ruled his people,
The city and the ring-riches. Indeed all his boast
The son of Beanstan had made good against you.
Therefore I expect, in spite of your ardency
In battle-shocks everywhere, in the bitter war-day,
Your fate will be worse if you dare to keep
Your all-night vigil in Grendel's path.'
    Beowulf spoke, Ecgtheow's son:
'Now Unferth my friend, you have given us a boxful   530
Of words about Breca, but surely it is the beer in you
Which has voiced his exploit? The truth is this:
It was I who had greater strength in the sea,
Peril in its surges, than any man beside.
It was something the two of us said as boys,
Boasting together – we were then both
Still in our teens – how we should venture

14

Our lives upon the ocean; and this we did.
We had naked swords, iron to our hands,
When we swam out to sea; we looked to defend ourselves   540
Against whale and killer. Not an inch of distance
Could he swim from me in the choppy waterway,
Swifter over the main; never would I leave him.
And so we two were on the sea together
The space of five nights, when a current split us,
A churning of the waters, in the chillest of weathers,
Blackness louring and north wind bending
Hostile against us; the waves were a chaos.
The temper of the sea-fish was stirred and irritated;
My chain-mail then, strong-linked, hand-locked,   550
Furnished me protection in the face of these enemies,
My ring-woven war-dress clung to my breast
Gold from the forge. A raging attacker
Dragged me to the bottom, savage, had me
Fast in his grasp; yet it was given me
To reach and to pierce the monstrous thing
With the point of my battle-sword; storm of conflict
Took the strong beast of the sea by this hand.
So time and again malicious tormentors
Heavily harassed me; and them I served   560
With this good sword, in the law of arms.
By no means did they, agents of hatred,
Enjoy that feasting where I should be fed on,
Sat round as a banquet at the bottom of the sea,
But when morning came they were washed and grounded,
Mauled by the sword, on the sands of the shore,
Sword-blade-silenced so that never again
Did they hinder seafarers making their voyage
On the deep acres. Light left the east,
God's bright beacon, and the floods subsided,   570
Until I could gaze on headlands, cliffs
Open to the winds. Fate often saves
The undoomed fightingman when his courage stands!
– Be that as it may, my sword succeeded
Against nine krakens. Never have I heard of
A harder fight under night and heaven

Or in streaming ocean a more desperate man;
Yet I kept my life from the haters' hold
In the weariness of my going. And so the sea
Drove me, the flood-tide, the milling waters   580
To the land of the Finns. Never did I hear
That you were in any such mortal encounters,
Such sword-blade-terrors. Breca never yet,
Nor you yourself either, in the play of war-weapons
With glancing sword fought out an exploit
So boldly (not that I pause to boast of it) –
Though you did slay your own brothers,
Your own close kinsmen, for which in hell
You shall endure damning, for all your intelligence.
It's the truth I tell you, son of Ecglaf,   590
That Grendel would never have laid such a train
Of terrors for your prince, the fiend-of-frightfulness
Such shame on Heorot, had your own mind been,
Your own heart as war-keen as you yourself claim;
But he has discovered he need not greatly
Fear the hostility, the deadly sword-fury
Of your people here, the Scylding men;
His toll he extorts, not one he spares
Of the Danish folk, but wars on them at will,
Killing, drowning, deeming the Danes   600
Incapable of opposing. But I soon now
Will show him in conflict what the Geats possess
Of strength and courage. Again let any
Go carefree to the mead when the morning-light,
The flame-mailed sun shines from the south,
Tomorrow's day on the children of men!'
    That was happiness to the giver of treasure,
Grey-haired, war-famed; the lord of the Danes
Saw help approaching; the protector of his people
Discovered in Beowulf steadfast intent.   610
There rose the laughter of men, the rejoicing
Resounded loudly, and speech was sweet.
Wealhtheow, Hrothgar's queen, came forward
Careful of the courtesies, gold-brilliant, welcomed
The men in the hall; and the royal hostess

First gave the cup to the guardian of the Danes,
Wished him, dear to his people, gladness
At the beer-banquet; and he took in happiness,
King of victories, hall-cup and feast.
The woman of the Helmings then went round   620
The whole of the retinue, old and young,
Proffering princely cups, till at last
She brought the mead-beaker, she the queen
Ring-bright and distinguished of mind, to Beowulf;
She addressed the Geat, gave thanks to God
In words of wisdom for granting her wish
That she might put trust in some hero's help
Against the disasters. He took the cup,
The war-hardened fighter from Wealhtheow's hands,
And then he declared, in the vision of battle –   630
Beowulf spoke, Ecgtheow's son – :
'I had this in mind at the time I embarked,
Entered the ship with my company of men,
That I should assuredly accomplish the yearning
Of all your people, or else be destroyed
In a fiend's stranglehold. Bravery of chivalry
I shall follow to victory, or else in this mead-hall
Suffer the close of my living days.'
The woman was greatly pleased with those words,
With the Geat's war-vow; the folk-queen went   640
Gold-shining, cynosure, to sit by her lord.
　　Then there were again in the hall as before
The talk of heroes and the happiness of men,
The hum of an illustrious concourse, till presently
The son of Healfdene was minded to rest,
To retire to his bed; he knew that the truce
In that monster's war on the great hall lasted
From the time when their eyes first saw the sunlight
Till louring night and the forms of the gloomy
Vaults came gliding over man and world   650
Black beneath the clouds. The whole assembly
Rose up. And he turned then to the other,
Hrothgar to Beowulf, wished him good fortune,
Entrusted him with the wine-hall, and spoke these words:

'Never have I committed to any man before,
Since I could wield my hand and shield,
The Danish stronghold, till here now to you.
Keep now and guard the best of homes
In the memory of honour, blaze valour's power,
For the fierce be sleepless! Nothing you may desire   660
Will be lacking if you live through your desperate purpose.'
    Then Hrothgar went with his troop of retainers,
The protector of the Scyldings, out of the hall;
The war-leader was ready to be with Wealhtheow
His consort and queen. For the King of Kings
Had appointed a hall-guard, as men now knew,
To watch against Grendel: in a special serving
Of the Danish king was his vigil for the giant;
But still the Geat had steadfast trust
In his spirit and strength and in the grace of God.   670
He took off then his war-coat of iron,
His helmet from his head; gave his chased sword,
The choicest of blades, to a hall-attendant,
And told him to hold and guard the battle-gear.
Then the good warrior uttered vaunt and vow,
Beowulf of the Geats, before he went to rest:
'I do not count myself of feebler striking-force
In the works of war than what Grendel boasts;
Therefore not with a sword shall I silence him,
Deprive him of his life, though it lies in my power;   680
Of good arms he knows nothing, of fighting face to face,
Of the shattering of shields, though he stands renowned
For works of violence; but we two shall scorn
The sword tonight, if he dares to join
Weaponless battle, and then let God,
Let the holy Lord decree the glory,
To whichever side may please his wisdom.'
The man lay down then, the pillow embraced
The hero's face, and many about him,
Eager sea-venturers, bent to their hall-beds.   690
Not one of them thought he would ever again
Leave there to find his beloved land,
His folk or his fortress, where he once was bred;

For they knew how sudden death had already
Swept from the wine-hall more than too many
Of those Danish men. But the Lord wove them
Fortunate war-fates, solace and support
He gave the Weder-folk, so that they all
Destroyed their enemy through the strength of one,
By his powers alone. – The truth is shown, 700
The great hand of God time out of mind
Moving mankind.
     Gliding at midnight
Came the gloomy roamer. The soldiers were sleeping –
Those who were guarding the gabled building –
All except one. Men well knew
That that malefactor in the forbidding of the Creator
Was powerless to draw them down beneath the shades;
But he, wideawake with heart-pent fury
And anger for the ravager, awaited fight's fortune.
Now by the swirling bluffs from his wasteland 710
Grendel came stalking; he brought God's wrath.
His sin and violence thought to ensnare
One of our kind in that hall of halls.
He moved through the night till with perfect clearness
He could see the banquet-building, treasure-home of men
Gold-panelled and glittering. Not his first visit
Was this for attacking the house of Hrothgar;
In no day of his life before or after
Did he find hall-men or a hero more dangerous!
Up then to the building the man came prowling 720
Devoid of all delighting. The door, firm-iron-bound,
Flew at once ajar when he breached it with his fists;
The hall's mouth he tore wide open, enraged
And possessed by his evil. Quickly after this
The fiend stepped over the stone-patterned floor,
Moved with fury; there started from his eyes
Unlovely light in the very form of fire.
Many a soldier he saw in the hall,
The company of kinsmen all asleep together,
The young warrior-band; and his heart exulted, 730
He aimed to divide, before day came,

Monstrous in frightfulness, life from limb
In every man of them, now that he had hope
Of ravening to gluttonousness. But the fate was finished
That could keep him after that night carnivorous
On human kind. The kinsman of Hygelac
Watched in his strength to see how the killer
Would go about his work with those panic hand-grips.
Nor did the monster mean to be backward,
But flashed to seize at the first opportunity   740
A soldier from his sleep, tore him unopposed,
Gnashed flesh from bone, at veins drank blood,
Gulped down the feast of his wounds; in a trice
He had the last of the dead man devoured,
To the feet and the fingers. He stepped farther in,
Caught then with his hand the iron-purposed
Warrior in his bed, the fiend with his fist
Reached out to seize him; he quickly gripped
The spite-filled creature, and rose upon his arm.
As soon as evil's dalesman discovered   750
That never had he known a stronger hand-grasp
In any other man beneath the sun
Throughout earth's acres, his mind began
To fear for his flesh; by that he escaped
None the more readily! He strained to be off,
To strike den and dark, join the devil-covens;
His fate in that place was without a fellow
Among his days before. Then the good warrior,
The kinsman of Hygelac recalled what he had said
That evening, stood up, and grappled him close;   760
Joints cracked aloud; the giant moved off,
The man strode after him. The byword for malice
Was minded, if he could, to slip into the distance
To the shelter of the fens – saw his fingers' force
In the fierce man's fist holds. A bitter coming
The persecutor had of it when he made for Heorot!
The royal hall rang; to all the Danes,
To all the fortress-men, the brave, the warriors
Came panic horror. Both hosts-of-the-hall
Were in rage, in ferocity. The building reverberated.   770

20

It was more than a marvel that that wine-house
Stood up to the battle-darers, that the splendid walls
Didn't fall to the ground; but it had the solidity,
It was cleverly compacted both inside and out
With its bands of iron. Many were the mead-benches
Sumptuous with gold that were wrenched there from the floor,
Beside the antagonists in their epic fury.
– A thing undreamed of by Scylding wisdom
That any man could ever, in any manner,
Shatter it as it stood stately and horn-spanned,   780
By sleights disrupt it: till fire's embrace
Should become its furnace. A sound mounted up
Uncouth, unceasing: terror unparalleled
Fell upon the Danes, upon every soul of them
Who listened by the ramparts to the noise of crying,
To the God-hated howling a lay of horror,
Song of lost triumph, the hell-fettered man
In lament for pain. He held him fast
Who at that hour of this earthly life
Was master of manhood of all mankind.   790
   Nothing would make the protector of warriors
Let slaughter's emissary escape alive,
Nor would he reckon many days left to him
Of profit to any man. Then Beowulf's soldiers
Brandished here and there their ancient swords,
Anxious to defend the body of their lord,
Of the illustrious prince, as they might be able –
Ignorant of this, when they moved to fight,
Iron-minded men of arms,
Thinking to strike on every side,   800
To pierce to his spirit: that the lawless ravager
Was not to be reached by any war-blade,
Not by the choicest metal on earth,
For every sword-edge and weapon of victory
He had blunted by wizardry. – Wretched his future
Now at that hour of this earthly life
Cut off from breath: far had the uncanny
Soul to wander into fiends' dominions.
For then he discovered, who often before

21

Had in his transgressions tormented the mind 810
Of human kind, he God's antagonist,
That his own body would not obey him,
But the kinsman of Hygelac in undaunted encounter
Had him in his grasp; each was to the other
Abhorrent if alive. The appalling demon
Bore flesh-agony; on his shoulder became manifest
A monstrous wound, sinews quivering,
Tendons ripped open. To Beowulf was granted
Triumph in that fight; but to Grendel the flight
In distress to death by the looming marshlands, 820
To his joyless home; he had no more doubt
That the end of his life had arrived in sight,
The lease-date of his light. All the Danes' desire
Was met and fulfilled by bloodshed of that fight.
For he who before had come from afar
In wisdom and singlemindedness had purged Hrothgar's hall,
Saved it from persecution. The night's work pleased him,
His deeds had proved him. The man of the Geats
Had carried out his boast in the sight of the Danes,
Just as he had redeemed the sum of that misery, 830
That sorrow in hostility they suffered in the past
And had to suffer, under stress of compulsion,
No small affliction. It was in clear tokening
Of this that the warrior laid down the hand,
The arm and the shoulder – the visible whole
Claw-hold of Grendel – beneath the soaring roof.
And then in the morning, as minstrels retell,
Warrior with warrior walked about the gift-hall;
Chieftains of the people from far and near
Crossed remote tracts to stare on the marvel, 840
The footmarks of the fiend. Ungrievous seemed
His break with life to all those men
Who gazed at the tracks of the conquered creature
And saw how he had left on his way from that place –
Heart-fatigued, defeated by the blows of battle,
Death-destined, harried off to the tarn of krakens –
His life-blood-spoor. There the becrimsoned
Waters were seething, the dreadful wave-sweep

22

All stirred turbid, gore-hot, the deep
Death-daubed, asurge with the blood of war,   850
Since he delightless laid down his life
And his heathen soul in the fen-fastness,
Where hell engulfed him.
                              The veterans returned.
And many a youth, from that glad journey,
Home from the lake, rejoicing on horseback,
White-mounted warriors. Beowulf's powers
Were spoken of there; it was said repeatedly
Neither north nor south from sea to sea
Was there any other man throughout the earth's immensity
Under arching heaven better in the bearing   860
Of a shield to battle or fitter to command.
– Not that they cast any slur on their lord,
Grace-given Hrothgar; king and exemplar.
Sometimes the warriors let their dappled
Horses gallop and run in rivalry,
Wherever they saw the paths were pleasant
And known to be favourable. Then a king's retainer,
A man proved of old, evoker of stories,
Who held in his memory multitude on multitude
Of the sagas of the dead, found now a new song   870
In words well linked: the man began again
To weave in his subtlety the exploit of Beowulf,
To recite with art the finished story,
To deploy his vocabulary. He uttered everything
He had heard related concerning Sigemund
And his acts of valour, much of it unknown,
The strife of Waels' son, his far travels,
Things unfamiliar to the children of men –
Feuds, crimes – except to his Fitela,
When these were the themes he was moved to muse over,   880
Uncle to nephew, as indeed they were ever
Battle-companions in all conflicts;
They had killed with their swords an untold number
Of the race of giants. Men were not niggardly
Of their praise of Sigemund after he was dead:
His ruthless war-arm destroyed the dragon,

The treasure-hoard-guardian; a prince's son,
He adventured the audacious meeting alone
Below the grey stone, for he didn't have Fitela;
Yet his was the fortune to transfix with his sword   890
The strangely-made serpent, till the noble metal
Stabbed to the cave-wall; the dragon died stabbed.
The hero had valiantly brought it about
That he might take pleasure in his own choice
Of the hoard of riches; he loaded his boat,
Bore into its hold the flashing luxuries,
He the son of Waels; the firedrake dissolved.
    That was the most widely famed of wanderers
Throughout the nations, defender of warriors,
For acts of valour – and by that he had prospered –   900
Since battle-prowess lapsed from Heremod,
Both daring and power: Heremod among fiends,
Into devilish hands evilly sent headlong
Impelled to his end; surging anxiety
Trammelled him too long, he became to his people,
To all his retinue, a mortal burden –
As many a wise man often lamented
His ruthless coming in former days,
Having trusted to find him an unraveller of their sufferings,
Now sorry his royal blood should flourish,   910
And he be dynastic, have command of the folk,
Of fortress and treasure-hoard, kingdom of heroes,
Country of the Scyldings. – That man, the kinsman
Of Hygelac, became the dearer to all,
To friends and humanity; evil the other.
    Racing intermittently, they paced their horses.
On the dust-pale road. Soon the early sun
Was swept swiftly on. Many a retainer
Went in all boldness to the hall of halls
To be amazed by the spectacle; and the king himself,   920
The jewel-hoard-guardian, stepped from his bedroom,
Splendid, surrounded by a numerous company,
Manifest in the dignities, came to the mead-hall,
His queen with him and a host of ladies.
    Hrothgar spoke – he went up to the house,

Stood at the porch, saw the great roof
Golden-lustred and Grendel's hand – :
'For this sight now let thanks be given
To Almighty God! Much have I endured,
Sorrows, Grendel's hate; God works for ever   930
Wonder upon wonder, Guardian of glory.
It was not long ago I despaired of living
To see a remedy in all my days
For any of our afflictions – when the best of houses
Stood stained with blood, with battle-crimson – ,
To see driven away the grief of statesmen
All unsuspecting that the stronghold of the people
Might ever be defended against its enemies,
Against demons, against phantoms. A soldier has now
Accomplished through the power of God the action   940
Which all of us before were never able
With cunning to contrive. Ah indeed that woman
Whoever she is that bore to humanity
This son, can say if she is living still,
To her the Ancient of Days was gracious
In the birth of her child. And now, Beowulf,
Best of men, I shall in this life
Love you as my son; keep the new kinship
Clean from this day. You shall not lack
Any wish in the world that I can supply.   950
How often for less have I ordered a reward,
Treasure-honours for an inferior warrior,
One weaker in fight! You on your own account
Have guaranteed in deeds that your glory will remain
Throughout all time. May the Almighty
With good repay you, as till now he has done!'
   Beowulf spoke, Ecgtheow's son:
'We most willingly undertook the conflict,
The work of courage, boldly made trial
Of the stranger's strength. I would that you   960
Were able rather to gaze on the fiend
In his natural armour mortally outfought!
My desire was to bind him with utmost speed
In unyielding handholds to the bed of blood,

So that he must lie in the grip of my fists
Scuffling for life, unless his flesh gave way;
I was unable, in the will of God,
To stop his escape, clung to him too loosely,
A desperate opponent; the fiend moved off
Far too impetuously. But he left his hand 970
To have his life, he left behind him
Both arm and shoulder; though not by that
Did the miserable man secure any solace,
No longer for that will the malefactor live,
Crushed by his crimes, for pain has come
With its press and clutch he can never unlock,
With its final fetters; there he must wait,
Outlawed in his evil, for the main judgement,
To see what the Creator in glory will decree him.'
      The son of Ecglaf was more silent then 980
In speaking with boasting about martial actions,
When the nobles gazed up at that high roof
To the hand the hero's strong hand gained them,
The fingers of the fiend: each one at the tip,
Each of the nail-joints was like very steel,
The spur of the heathen fighter's fist,
The claw, was monstrous; every man said
Not the hardest blade, tested of old,
Would be able to touch him and so despoil
The walking horror of his bloody battle-arm. 990
      Then hands were ordered to be busy at once
Decorating Heorot; and many there were,
Both men and women, at work in the wine-hall,
The house of hospitality. Gold-woven tapestries
Glittered along the walls, many a curiosity
For the eyes of everyone gazing on such a thing.
Severely shattered was the shining building,
For all its inward iron-band-buttressing;
Its door-hinges were sprung; only roof escaped
Without any damage when the slaughter-guilty 1000
Deed-stained monster turned away in flight
Despairing of life. Difficult is the flight
From that, from fate – let any man attempt it – ,

For each human soul, each child of man,
Each earth-inhabitant inevitably urged
Has to take possession of a place prepared,
Where the body enlaired and in bed locked fast
Sleeps after its feast.
                    Now time had come
For the son of Healfdene to go to the hall;
The king himself was eager for the banquet.   1010
Never, I am sure, in a greater assembly
Did men show better than these with their treasure-giver.
Now at the bench the heroes were seated
And enjoyed their fill; and there the kinsmen,
Hrothgar and Hrothulf, great of heart
In that great hall, courteously quaffed
Many a mead-draught. Heorot was packed
With friendly men: no hint then
That folk of the Scyldings would try treachery!
The son of Healfdene gave now to Beowulf   1020
As victor's reward a gold-woven banner,
A patterned battle-pennant, a helmet, a mail-coat,
And a great sword of swords, brought to the warrior
In the sight of all. Beowulf took up
His cup in the hall; he had no need of shame
Before the fightingmen for that sumptuous gift;
Not many people have I heard of presenting
To others at the ale-bench in a friendlier way
A fourfold treasure finished in gold.
Round the helmet-top a wire-twisted crest   1030
Kept from outside the head's protection,
That the well-filed swords, the battle-tempered
Would glance, not bite, whenever the shieldsman
Should sally out against hostile men.
And the captain of heroes had eight horses
With gold-inlaid head-trappings brought in the hall,
In under that roof; one with a saddle
Marvellously decorated, made rich with jewels:
This was the war-mount of that great king
When the son of Healfdene had a mind to engage   1040
In the battle-play of swords – never did his famed

27

Fighting-strength fail him when the dead were falling
In the front of battle. And then the Danes' king
Entrusted to Beowulf both of these things,
The horses and the arms: in happiness to use them.
So, as a man should, the illustrious prince,
Wealth-guard of warriors; repaid the war-frays
With chargers and treasures such as none shall decry
Who is willing to speak of them in justice and truth.
Then still the king, to each of the men   1050
Who had made with Beowulf that ocean-voyage,
Gave at the mead-bench a costly present,
An heirloom-gift, and commanded the recompense
To be paid in gold for that man alone
Whom Grendel had wickedly killed before –
As more of them he would have, till God in his wisdom
And the man's courage forbade them that fate.
Everything human in the hand of God
Was and now is. Best therefore everywhere
Is intelligence, foresight. Much must he learn   1060
Both in love and in horror, who for long here
In these days of warring draws breath in the world!
    There before Healfdene's battle-commander
Voice and melody rose together,
Harp-joy plucked and lays related,
When Hrothgar's minstrel came along the mead-bench
To deliver his pleasure with words in the hall.
*[He told his hearers a tale of the Frisians,]
Of the men of Finn and the attack made on them.
– Hnaef of the Scyldings, hero of the Half-Danes,
Was fated to fall on a Frisian field;   1070
Nor had she Hildeburh cause to commend
The Jutes' good faith; guiltless she lost
In the play of war-shields those she loved,
Both son and brother; pierced by the spear
They dropped to their doom; that woman knew grief.
Not at all emptily was Hoc's daughter
Lamenting fate when morning came,
When her eyes could gaze on the carnage of kinsmen
Under heaven's sky, where once she had enjoyed

All earthly delight. War took away   1080
Finn's whole troop except a mere handful,
Making him helpless in that place of battle
To force the fighting an inch upon Hengest
And in combat crush for that prince's retainer
His last-ditch survivors; but they offered them terms:
To clear for them completely another hall-building,
With a throne of honour, and they to share
Possession of half with the men of the Jutes,
The son of Folcwalda at the givings of riches
Honouring the Danes, entertaining Hengest   1090
And his men with ring-presents – with precious treasures
Of beaten gold – on every occasion
And just as freely as his hand encouraged
His Frisian folk in the beer-banquet-hall.
Then they concluded on the two sides
A firm pledge of peace. Finn to Hengest
Bound himself by oaths strongly and unreservedly:
To protect with honour, by authority of his council,
The survivors in their misery, and no man there
Was to break that pledge by either word or deed,   1100
Nor must they murmur with malicious mind
Though it was their ring-giver's killer they followed,
Deprived of their prince, as compulsion forced them;
And if any Frisian with hotheaded talk
Should provoke recollection of the feud and its blood
Then the edge of the sword would provoke it after.
– The pyre was prepared, and ancient gold
Taken from the treasure-hoard. The best of soldiers
Among Scylding men was ready for the flames.
Beside that pyre, needing no seeking,   1110
Were the blood-stained chain-shirt, the gold-cased boar-device,
The iron-hard tusk-emblem, and many a fine man
Dead of wounds, fallen, as some fell, in the fighting.
Hildeburh called then for her own son
To be committed to the burning at the pyre of Hnaef
And his body consumed, to be laid on the faggots
At his uncle's shoulder. The woman mourned,
In dirges lamented them. The warrior was lifted;

The greatest of death-fires swirled to the clouds,
Roared before the mound; heads ran molten,   1120
Wound-lips cracked, cruel flesh-tearings,
Jetted out their blood; the blaze, insatiablest
Of spirits, devoured all the war dead
Present on both sides: from the pride of life.
– So the fighters went back, bereft of friends,
To make for their dwellings, to go to Friesland,
To their upland town and homes. But Hengest
Still stayed with Finn out of hard necessity
That death-tainted winter. He pictured his country,
Powerless as he was to put out to sea   1130
The ring-prowed boat – the ocean storm-churned,
Battling with the wind, winter-wave-bound
In chain of ice, till another season
Visited the world, as it must, with days
Gloriously adazzle in vigil for their hours
For ever without fail. Winter passed then,
Fair was earth's face; the exile hated,
The stranger, these courts; but considered more
The avenging of sorrow than the voyaging of the seas,
How he might bring about a battle-meeting   1140
For his inward brooding over Jutish men.
So his became the remedy of a common desire,
And he took up in his arms the sword of swords,
The blade Hunlafing, flashing in war;
Its edges were not unknown to the Jutes.
So also there fell on the bold-heart Finn
Fierce sword-killing at his own home again,
When Guthlaf and Oslaf complained of their misery
And the savage assault made on the seafarers,
Charged him with their many griefs: restless   1150
The hearts in their breasts could forbear no more.
The hall then was crimsoned with lifeblood of fighters,
And Finn himself slain, the king among his host,
And the queen taken. The Scyldings transferred
To their ships all the furnishings of that country's king,
And whatever they could find in the house of Finn –
Rare gems and jewels. The noble lady

They carried by sea in their voyage to the Danes,
Brought her to her people.
    So the lay was sung,
The story of the minstrel. The glad stir resumed, 1160
Loud rang the bench-clamour, cupbearers poured
From kingly wine-jugs. Then moved forward
Wealhtheow diademed with gold to where the two good warriors
Were sitting, uncle with nephew; at that time peace still bound them,
Each was true to the other. Spokesman Unferth there too
Sat at the Scylding king's feet; every man believed in his integrity,
That he possessed a mind of power, although he had been
        unmerciful
To his kinsmen when swords were glancing. Then the woman of the
        Scyldings spoke:
    'Take this cup, my own lord and king,
    Giver of treasure. Take your pleasure 1170
    Gold-friend of men, and speak to the Geats
    With words of kindness as courtesy commands.
    To the Geats be gracious, magnanimous to proffer
    What you here possess from far and near.
    You I believe have asked the warrior
    To be as your son. Heorot is cleansed,
    This glorious gift-hall; be free while you can
    With rewards unstinted, and leave to your kinsmen
    People and kingdom when you have to embark
    In the vision of doom. I have faith in Hrothulf, 1180
    Good as he is, that he will honourably
    Keep the young retinue, if you before he,
    Friend of the Scyldings, should leave the world;
    Surely he will with liberality
    Repay our own sons, remembering everything
    We did for him as a child, kindnesses of old,
    To give him delight and lay honours upon him.'
She turned to the bench then, where her sons were,
Hrethric and Hrothmund, and all the young retainers
The children of heroes; the good warrior sat there 1190
Beowulf of the Geats beside the two brothers.
The cup was brought to him, and friendly words
Invited him to drink, and twisted gold

Was gladly offered him, two arm-ornaments,
War-chains and rings, and the greatest necklace
I have ever known of here on this earth.
– No better treasure from human hoard
Was seen beneath the sun since Hama bore off
The Brosing necklace to that brilliant city,
Gem, mount, and lustre; he fled from Eormenric's   1200
Crafty machinations, chose timeless wisdom.
The next possessor of that ring-jewel
Was Hygelac of the Geats, Swerting's grandson,
From the time when his banner guarded the treasure,
Defended the war-booty; he was seized by fate
When for glory's sake he courted misery
In Frisians' enmity. Those jewels he took,
The powerful prince, those rare stones over
The brimming waves; and by his shield he fell.
The king's body passed then into Frankish hands,   1210
His coat of mail, and the necklace as well;
Worse were the warriors who after that battle-slaughter
Plundered the dead; Geat folk filled
The field of the killed. – The hall-rafters rang.
Wealhtheow spoke, she said before the company:
'Take joy in this jewel, and prosper, Beowulf,
Young man endeared to us, and be served by the chainmail
And by these great treasures, and flourish, flourish,
Show yourself in your strength, and be to these boys
Kind in your counsel. Reward for that kindness   1220
Will be in my mind. What you have accomplished
Means men will praise you both far and near
Whenever and wherever the sea beats round
Earth's blustering cliffs. Warrior be happy
While life is yours! May you from my wishes
Grow rich in treasures. Be good to my son,
Act in charity from your store of joy.
Here every man is true to his fellow,
Humane of mind and loyal to his lord,
The retinue are as one, the people are eager,   1230
The heroes are wine-glad and quick to my beckon.'
    She went then to her seat. Men drank their wine:

Best of feasts there! Of fate they knew nothing,
Of destiny to be dreaded, of what was to fall
Upon many a man when evening came
And Hrothgar retired to his own dwelling,
The prince to his rest. A multitude of warriors
Were on guard in the hall, as they often were before.
They cleared the bench-floor; soon it was spread
With beds and bolsters. Many a beer-banqueter   1240
Bent to his hall-couch for sleep – and no waking.
They placed by their heads their shining shields
Their battle-bucklers; and there on the bench
Above the heroes, not far to seek:
Woven chain-mail, crown-of-war helmet,
Terrible spear-shaft! Their custom it was
To be ready for war at any time,
Both at home and on service, and in each of these
On whatever occasions their own liege lord
Should find himself at hazard: an excellent people.   1250

[1251–1887] *Beowulf and Grendel's Mother*

They sank then to sleep. For his night's rest
One paid heavily, as had often been
Their lot since Grendel haunted the gold-hall,
Acted his evil till the end was obtained,
Death for his sins. It was soon clear to men,
Known far and wide, that an avenger still
Had survived the enemy, survived for some time
The agony of the battle: that misery was remembered
By the mother of Grendel, monster in woman-sex,
She who had to live in the terrible streams,   1260
The freezing waters, when Cain became
The sword-blade-slayer of his own brother
The fruit of his father, and then went outlawed,
Fled murder-branded from joy of mankind,
Made wilderness his home: from him sprang thick
Demons of God's doom, Grendel among them
Man-hated, homicidal, the finder in Heorot

33

Of a fighter vigilant and waiting for war;
The monster had him there in his grip,
But he called to mind the strength he commanded,   1270
The magnificent gift God had granted him,
And he looked to the Lord for all his grace,
For his solace and support; and defeated the fiend,
Humbled the hell-fetch. Wretched he went then,
Devoid of all delighting, to seek death in hiding,
Enemy of humanity. But now his mother,
Blackhearted and gluttonous, was moved to set out
On a journey of danger to avenge her son's death.

    To Heorot then she came, where the Danes
Slept within the hall. Fate for those men   1280
Swept on its wheel when Grendel's mother
Got into the building. The panic was the less
By just as much as the strength of woman-sex,
Amazon battle-fury, is less than a man's
When the band-adorned sword, hammer-hardened,
The bloodstained blade unyielding of edge
Bites on the boar-image of a hostile head.
Then in the hall the tough-tempered sword
Was drawn above the benches, and many a broad shield
By firm hand lifted; when that horror clutched,   1290
Who thought of helmet or of great chain-mail?
She was off in haste, anxious to leave there,
To escape with her life, when men discovered her;
She had fastened in a flash on one of the heroes
With heavy grasp, and gone to her fen.
He whom she tore from sleep to death
Was held by Hrothgar as the dearest of men
Raised among retainers from sea to sea,
Fine shield-fighter, soldier of good name.
Beowulf was absent, for a separate lodging   1300
Had earlier been prepared, after the treasure-giving,
For the illustrious Geat. Clamour in Heorot!
She had taken that sight, the bloodied hand;
Care came again, fell on those dwellings.
Evil the barter where both sides must tender
The lives of their friends!

                                  The aged king
The grey-haired warrior was vexed in his mind,
When he learned that his leading retainer lay
Lifeless, that his dearest man was dead.
Speedily Beowulf the victorious soldier
Was summoned to the room. As day was breaking
This man went in, the noble fighter
And his companions with him, where the wise king waited
Wondering if the Lord would ever grant him
A happy reversal of his wretched history.
Then the trusted warrior walked across the floor
With his own band of men – the hall-wood reverberated –
Until he approached and spoke to the wiseminded
Ruler of the Danes, asked if he had had
An untroubled night according to his desire.
    Hrothgar spoke, protector of the Scyldings:
'About happiness ask nothing! Sorrow has returned
To the Danish people. Aeschere is dead,
The elder brother of Yrmenlaf,
Counsellor and adviser close to my heart,
Shoulder-comrade in the days of war
When we guarded our heads as troops clashed
And struck at boar-emblems. As Aeschere was,
Seasoned and trusted, so should man be.
A wandering spirit bloodthirsty in Heorot
Killed him with her hands; where she went back to,
Gladdened by her feasting, glorying in the carrion,
Horrible – is unknown to me. The fight she has avenged
Where yesterday evening you destroyed Grendel
In violent act with unlax fists
Since he had deprived me of my folk and ruined them
Longer than was right. He fell in the strife,
His life he forfeited, and now this demon
Has come in her power to avenge her kin –
And has done much already to retaliate in the feud,
As may now appear to many a retainer
Grieving in his mind for the giver of treasure:
Heavy the heartache, now that that hand
Is at rest which availed for all your desires.

This I have heard my people say,
Country-dwellers and statesmen in hall,
Two they had seen, two such, huge,
The moors their kingdom, wasteland-stalkers,
Unearthly creatures. One of them had,
As far as they were able with certainty to discern,   1350
The form of a woman; her joyless companion
Took in man's shape his outcast steps –
Except that he was greater than any man besides;
And from long long ago to people of this land
Grendel is his name; as for their paternity –
The souls are occult that might have been ancestors
In earlier days! They guard a region
Uncouth, wolves' dunes, blustering headlands,
Desperate fen-ground, where the mountain-torrent
Falls down under the louring bluffs,   1360
Pours down to earth. It is not far distant
Measured by miles that that lake lies;
Groves overhang it clothed with hoarfrost,
A great-rooted wood throws shade on its water.
There a strange horror at night may be seen,
A blaze on the stream. Of the children of men
Not one has wisdom that could plumb that abyss.
Even when the strong-horned stag, the heath-prancer
Hard-pressed by hounds, hunted from afar,
Is searching for a covert, sooner will he die,   1370
Give up his life at the lake-edge, than enter
To hide his head there. Unholy that place is:
Up from it mounts the tumult of waters
Black to the clouds, when the wind rouses
Malice and tempest darkening the air
Till the weeping of the skies. – Now help again
Is in your hands alone. The land is still new to you,
The desperate spot that awaits your encounter
With its vicious denizen; let your daring take you!
I shall repay you for that fight with riches,   1380
With long-guarded treasures, as I did before,
With twisted gold, if you return once more.'
    Beowulf spoke, Ecgtheow's son:

'Wise lord, leave grief! Better for every man
Is the avenging of his friend than long sorrowing.
Each of us has to abide the ending
Of life in the world; let him strive who can
For glory before death, because that is best
To the retainer after his life is spent.
Rise up king of men, let us quickly set off   1390
And examine the track of Grendel's kinswoman.
This I promise you: she shall relish no retreat,
Neither the bowels of the earth nor the mountain forest
Nor the bottom of the sea, go where she will!
You now, for all the distresses you bear
Be patient this day, as I look for you to be.'
    The old king leapt up, gave thanks to God,
To the Lord in his power, for what the man had spoken.
Hrothgar's horse then was bitted and bridled,
The wavy-maned mount. The wise-minded prince   1400
Rode off in his armour; a troop of shieldsmen
Marched at his side. There lay the footmarks
Visible far and wide through the woodland paths,
The track across the plains, the way she had headed
Over the gloomy moor, carrying off lifeless
That best of retainers, the chief of those
Who kept with Hrothgar watch in the hall.
Then the children of men passed over
Precipitous rock-falls, narrow pathways,
Dangerous defiles, a road unmapped,   1410
Abrupt promontories riddled with kraken-caves;
He with a handful of wary-minded men
Rode on in front scanning the country,
Till he came suddenly upon the mountain-trees
Bending low over hoary rock,
A joyless forest; beneath lay the water
Labouring and blood-thickened. To the Scylding company,
To all the Danes came vexation of heart
Hard to be borne, to many a retainer,
To every man grief when they found   1420
On the cliffs of the lake, Aeschere's head.
Waves welled blood as the people looked,

Boiled with crimson. At intervals the horn
Sang its sharp troop-summons. Foot-soldiers sat then
And saw over the water serpentkind congregated,
Strange sea-dragons making trial of the tarn,
Krakens too, lying on the headland slopes,
Like those which often in morning forays
Gally the mariners' thoroughfare,
Reptiles, wild creatures. They backed away   1430
Irritated, angered; they recognized the blast,
The war-horn-song. A man of the Geats
With his bow cut one of them off from life,
From warring with the waves, a hard battle-arrow
Boring into its lifeblood; it was the slacker in swimming
Over the ocean after death seized it.
At once it was closely cornered in the waves
By keen-barbed boar-pikes, forcibly taken
And drawn up on the headland, an amazing denizen
Of wave and flood; the men gazed at it,   1440
Grisly thing and uncouth!
                  Beowulf put on
The garments of battle, of his own life heedless;
The broad war-corslet designed with art,
Close-hand-woven, must probe the water,
War-corslet expert to protect his body,
Lest battlehold of the enraged, lest malicious clutch
Might have power to attain his heart and his life;
And his head was guarded by that gleaming helmet
Which must trouble and stir the abysses of the lake,
Visit the mulling of streams, bejewelled,   1450
Chain-circled, princelike, just as long ago
The weapon-smith made it, marvellously forged it,
Set boar-figures round it, that never thereafter
Might sword or war-metal be able to shear it.
That too was not the meagrest of mainstays
Which Hrothgar's spokesman lent him at need:
Hrunting was the name of that hefted sword;
It was one famous among ancient treasures;
The blade was of iron, poison-twig-patterned,
Battle-blood-hardened; never did it fail   1460

Any man at war who grasped it in his hands,
Who dared adventure in exploits of danger,
In the homestead of fighters; not for the first time
Was it now to accomplish an act of valour.
The son of Ecglaf strong in power
Was indeed forgetful of what he said before
With wine in his words when he lent that weapon
To a finer swordsman; himself fearful
Of venturing his life under the waves' uproar,
To manifest his heroism: losing glory so,   1470
Fame of good acts. With the other how different
Once he had put on the garments of battle!
    Beowulf spoke, Ecgtheow's son:
'Recall now, illustrious heir of Healfdene,
Wise prince, now that I am ready to go,
Gold-friend of men, what we two have said,
That if I in your service should lose my life
You would stand always in the place of a father
To me after I had gone from the world.
Embrace in your protection my young retainers,   1480
My comrades-in-arms, if war should take me;
Also send Hygelac, Hrothgar my friend,
Those precious things you have made me a gift of,
And the lord of the Geats may in that gold perceive,
Hrethel's son see when he gazes on that treasure,
That I found a ring-giver noble in all kingly
Liberalities, and enjoyed them while I was able.
And let Unferth have the ancient heirloom,
Let the far-famed man have the hard-edged sumptuous
Wave-scrolled sword; I with Hrunting   1490
Shall win my glory, or death shall take me.'
    After these words the man of the Geats
Hastened off eagerly – by no means lingering
For any rejoinder; the surging water
Closed over the warrior. It was almost a day then
Before he could make out the form of the lake-floor.
She at once, guardian of the field of floods
For a century of seasons, savage-ravenous,
Grim and gluttonous, discovered some man

Was sounding there, down towards dominions of
    demon-kind.   1500
She grappled with him then, gripped the warrior
In frightful fistholds; hurting none the sooner
The firm flesh within – the casing chain-armour
Kept him round about, the war-dress unpierced,
The interlocked mail-coat by her fierce fingers.
When the wolfish water-fiend reached the bottom
She carried the ring-giver, the prince, to her hall,
So that he couldn't – whatever his bravery –
Make use of his weapons, and then through the water
Countless strange things harassed him, sea-beasts   1510
Of many kinds tried with their battle-tusks to slash
His chain-mail, monsters tormented him. Then the man
Saw he was in some hall of his enemy's,
Where not a drop of water would harm him,
Where a vaulted chamber kept the sudden
Flood-fall from touching him; and he saw firelight,
A gleam and a flashing brilliantly shining.
    The good fighter saw then the abyss's curse,
The great sea-demon-woman; a tremendous onslaught
He made with his war-sword, his hand drove its stroke,   1520
Till the ring-banded blade rang out on her head
Its hungry battle-song. Then the stranger found
That the glittering metal refused to bite,
Would not hurt life, but the edge failed
The prince in his need; it had borne brunt before
Of many an encounter, hacked many a helmet
And doomed man's war-dress; for the precious treasure
This was the first time its glory faltered.
    Resolute again was Hygelac's kinsman,
Not backward in bravery, mindful of all audacity.   1530
The warrior now infuriated threw down on the ground
The wave-marked sword steel-edged and stubborn
With its bands of rare handiwork; he put faith in strength,
In the hand-grip of power. So shall a man act
When in the midst of war he takes heart to win
Long-living praise: careless of his life
The man of the Geats then seized by the shoulder –

No shrinking in that fight! – Grendel's mother,
And roused by rage to battle-relentlessness
Swung the desperate enemy till she fell to the floor.   1540
She in turn quickly gave him a requital
With her cruel clawholds and closely grappled him;
Then the foot-soldier, strongest of warriors,
Exhausted in spirit, slipped and fell,
And she bestrode her hall-guest, and drew her knife
Broadbladed, burnished; vengeance she wanted
For her child, her only son. On his shoulder lay
The chain-net of his war-mail protecting his flesh,
Forbidding the piercing of spear-point and sword-edge.
The son of Ecgtheow and champion of the Geats   1550
Would then have been lost under the vastness of the earth
If his coat of armour had not furnished him help,
His unyielding battle-mail – and God in holiness
Drawn the fight to triumph: in his wisdom the Lord
The Ruler of the heavens gave his simple
Decree for the right, when he rose once more.
Then he saw a sword, a victor among weapons,
A blade of old time, giant-forged, tough-edged,
An honour for its bearers; it was the best of arms,
Only greater in bulk than could ever be carried   1560
By any other man into press of battle,
Trustworthy, a splendour, the labour of titans.
The chained hilt he seized then, the Scyldings' champion
In fierceness and war-anger, brandished the ringed blade
Despairing of life, and in fury struck,
So that it bit hard into her neck
Till the backbone broke: the iron pierced through
A doomed shell of flesh; she dropped to the floor;
The sword was bloodstained, the man's work gladdened him.
     Radiance flashed out, the light sprang within,   1570
Twin to the candle of heaven as in clearness
It shines from the sky. Hygelac's retainer
Looked along the vault, turned by the wall,
Lifted up the weapon firmly by its hilt,
Angry and unrelenting – the warrior didn't count
That swordblade despicable, but was eager to be quick

41

In repaying Grendel for the multitude of attacks
He had made warring on the Danish nation
Oftener by far than on that one occasion
When he slaughtered Hrothgar's hearth-companions   1580
Lying at their rest, devoured fifteen
Folk of the Danes, slumbering men,
And went carrying off as many more again,
Plunderings of horror. For that he had rewarded him,
The fierce-minded fighter, so that now he could gaze on
Grendel lying moveless, war-drained of his force,
Lifeless, as the battle in hours gone
Had crushed him in Heorot. The corpse burst open,
When he suffered a blow even after death,
A keen sword-stroke; so he beheaded him.   1590
    Immediately the wise-hearted men who were looking
With Hrothgar at the water saw that its waves
In their streaming tumult were all stirred turbid,
That the flood was blood-flecked. The grey-streaked heads,
The old men drew together speaking of the good warrior,
How they thought the prince would never return,
Come back in victory to visit again
The illustrious king; it was what many feared then,
That the wolfish sea-demon-woman had been his destruction.
Now it was the ninth hour of the day. The valiant   1600
Scyldings left the cliff; the gold-lord of men
Turned from there to his home. The strangers sat
Sick at heart and stared across the lake;
They desired and they despaired to look on the living flesh
Of their lord and friend. Then that sword, that war-blade
Bloodied by the fight began wasting away
In battle-icicles: it was a thing to marvel at
When it all melted down as if it was the ice
The Father unleashes from the chain of frost,
Water-bonds he slips whose power keeps   1610
All times and seasons; he in truth is God.
The man of the Geats took no more from that place
In the way of rich possessions (though he saw plenty there)
Than the head of Grendel and with it that hilt
Bristling with jewels; the sword had dissolved,

The scrolled blade fused: so hot that blood was,
So venomous the hell-fiend who died in that hall.
Quickly he swam off; he had fought before to see
His enemies war-felled; he thrust up through the water.
Cleansed were the tumult and swirl of the waves, 1620
Pure the vast reaches, when the alien soul
Left living days and this lease of creation.
    The protector of seafarers came then to land,
Swimming resolutely; he rejoiced in the sea-booty,
In the weighty burden he carried with him.
The splendid retinue went then to meet him,
They gave thanks to God, they were gladdened by the prince
Now that their eyes could see him unharmed.
Then the brave warrior's helmet and chain-mail
Were speedily loosened. The tarn lay still, 1630
The water with death's red stained under the sky.
They followed the footpaths forward from that place,
They were happy at heart, they marched across the earth,
On the well-known road; noble in valour
Men took the head from the lake-side cliff,
And every one of them, a soldier and distinguished,
Found the task hard; four of them were needed,
And trouble was needed, to bear on the spear-shaft
Grendel's head to the hall of gold,
Till presently the men, the fourteen Geats 1640
War-keen and daring came up to the house;
The lord of the retinue, soldierly among his throng,
Walked with them along the mead-hall's approaches.
And so the prince of warriors came in,
The man bold of act, the battle-brave hero
In glory revered, to greet Hrothgar.
Then Grendel's head was brought by the hair
Into the hall where the retinue were drinking,
A horror before the nobles and the woman with them,
A spectacle and a wonder; men's eyes were transfixed. 1650
    Beowulf spoke, Ecgtheow's son:
'O Scylding prince, heir of Healfdene,
These sea-spoils which you look on here
We have brought you in gladness as the token of conquering.

43

Not easily did I escape with my life
In that submarine strife, my daring in the deed
Was done under difficulty; the combat would immediately
Have been swept to a close, but God shielded me.
Nothing in the battle could I accomplish
With Hrunting, although it is a weapon of power; 1660
But grace was granted me by the Lord of men –
He surest guide of those made friendless –
To see hung on the wall, beautiful, huge,
A sword of old time; and this blade I drew.
The hall's guard was killed when time and chance
Became mine in that fight. The wave-scrolled war-sword
Burnt away then as the blood burst out,
Ferventest battle-sweat. From there I plundered,
From the enemy, that hilt; I avenged the crimes,
The carnage of the Danes, as it was mine to do. 1670
Now this I promise you, that you in Heorot
May sleep without sorrow among your retainers
As may all your people from veteran to boy:
That you need have fear of death and ill
For them, for your men, prince of the Scyldings,
Never from that quarter where you feared before.'
Then into the hands of the year-worn warrior
Was the golden hilt given, titan-work of old
To the grey-haired battle-leader; it came into the possession
Of the lord of the Danes when the demons fell, 1680
Master-smiths' wonder-work; when God's adversary,
The man black of heart, murder-sin-stained
And his mother with him went from the world,
It passed into the power of the best of kings
Ruling on earth from sea to sea
Who ever distributed treasures in Denmark.
    Hrothgar spoke; he gazed on the hilt,
On the ancient heirloom inscribed with the genesis
Of that far-off strife when the ocean, the pouring
Flood struck down all giantkind; 1690
Audacity was in their acts, they were a race estranged
From God everlasting: rewarded for it at last
When the rising waters were stirred by the Lord.

Also on the hilt-plates of glittering gold
Was carefully charactered in runic letters,
Written and expressed for whom the good blade,
The spiral-hafted sword, the serpent-patterned
Had first been made. Now in his wisdom spoke
Healfdene's son – all were silent – :
'Ah, the old guardian of his country who has dealt   1700
In sincerity and justice with his folk, recalling
All things, far back, may well say this man
Was born for excelling! Beowulf my friend,
Through remote regions over every nation
Your power and renown are raised. You hold it all in watchfulness,
Your strength with wariness of mind. I shall bind fast with you
That friendship we spoke of before. You shall live to be a comfort
To your own people through long years,
A blessing to men. – How different was Heremod
To Ecgwela's folk, to Scylding retainers!   1710
He grew not to their pleasure but rather to the slaughter
And the bloody murder of the Danish people;
He destroyed in his wrath his banquet-companions
And his bosom-comrades, till he turned away in exile,
A prince and a byword, from all human happiness.
Although mighty God had advanced him in virtues
Of strength and vigour, had set him at the forefront
Of all other men, his heart began to harbour
Bloodthirsty purposes; not a ring would he give
To the Danes for his glory; he lived without joy   1720
Till he came to atone for the distress and the strife,
His folk's long-suffering. Make this your wisdom,
Show man free-hearted! It is for your ears
I have told this lay, from the store of my years.
                              It is strange to consider how mighty God
In his vast meditation endows mankind –
Rank, lands, intelligence: all from his power.
Sometimes in a man of illustrious race
He allows the understanding to meander into delight,
Proffers him in his own place the pleasures of the world   1730
And the fortress-city of his folk to serve him,
Makes a great kingdom, great tracts of the earth

45

Seem his to keep, till he cannot see
In his own unwisdom that it will ever end.
His life is a feasting; neither sickness nor decrepitude
Cripples him with one touch, nor does any battle-sorrow
Spread black through his heart, nor contention anywhere
In sword-hatred bear fruit, but the whole world
Wheels towards his will; he knows nothing of the reverse,
Till in his own mind a monstrous arrogance   1740
Swells and flourishes while the watchman drowses,
The soul's keeper – O sleep too clinging,
Fettered by his cares, and that killer so near
Who strikes from his bow satanic bolts!
Then in his armour he feels his breast shot
By a stinging shaft – guard himself he cannot – ,
By strange cross-promptings from the accursed spirit;
What he has long possessed seems to him too little,
He turns miser, heart-malign, never offers for his honour
The gold-rich ring-treasures, and the doom to come   1750
Is oblivion in him and blindness, because God once gave him,
God the king of Glory, distinctions and greatness.
But the end is written and it comes to pass
That the brittle shell of flesh perishes,
In its fate falls; and another rules
To dispense precious things, hero-wealth of old,
With a reckless hand, regardless of fear.
Guard yourself against that malignity and ill,
Beloved Beowulf, best of men,
And grasp what is fairer, the faith everlasting;   1760
Glorious warrior, abhor every vainglorying.
In this brief hour the flower of your manhood
Blows, and then in a flash either sickness or the sword,
Either the seizure of fire or the seething of the flood,
Either battle-blade's bite or battle-spear's flight
Or terrible decrepitude shall deprive you of life,
Or the light of your eyes shall dwindle and darken;
O prince, in what imminent death are you stricken!
    I myself have ruled the Danes under the sun
For half a century, and I protected them against   1770
Assault from many a tribe widespread on this earth,

46

Against spear and sword, till I counted myself free
Of every adversary beneath the arch of heaven.
Ah, how that was changed for me and my country,
From solace to sorrow, once Grendel the inveterate
Antagonist became my invader here;
Great grief of mind I bore incessantly
From that persecution. Let God be thanked,
The eternal Lord, that I should ever have lived
To gaze with my own eyes, after this ancient feud,   1780
On that head stained with the blood of the sword.
Now take your seat and have pleasure in the feast,
Honoured by your war-deeds; it is unnumbered treasures
I shall be sharing with you when morning comes.'
    The Geat rejoiced, he went at once
To take up his place as the wise king required.
Then as once before the guests sitting in hall,
The fighters of courage were feasted courteously
For a second time. Shade from night's shell
Fell dark on the retinue. The nobles arose;   1790
The grey-haired man, the aged Scylding
Was ready for his rest. The Geat, the brave shieldsman
Looked forward to his sleep more than he could say;
At once the far-traveller tired after his adventure
Was shown to his place by a hall-attendant,
By one whose duty it was to look after
Each need of a warrior, such as in those days
Seafaring soldiers might happen to have.
The great-hearted man took his rest; the building
Soared up, huge-vaulted, gold-shimmering; its guest   1800
Slept on within till the swarthy raven
Gave happy greeting to the glory of heaven.
Then light shook out bright above the shadows;
The fighters sprang up, the warriors were eager
To make again for home; the spirit of the stranger
Strained to see his ship and leagues of its wake.
The bold soldier called then for Hrunting to be brought
To the son of Ecglaf, had him take his sword,
Priceless metal; thanked him for its use,
Saying he had proved it a friend in battle,   1810

War-tough, excellent – his words found no fault
In that blade's edge. A man who knew courage!
And at last the warriors, the voyage-desirers
Were ready in their armour; the prince dear to the Danes
Went up to the throne where the other prince was,
The valorous fightingman saluted Hrothgar,
Beowulf spoke, Ecgtheow's son:
   'The time has come for us seafarers,
Far-borne visitors, to say we are departing
On our way to Hygelac. This place has been hospitable   1820
Unfailingly and to all desire; you have done us every favour.
If now on this earth I can earn by any means
A mightier portion of your mind's love
Than I yet have won in the works of war,
O lord of men, I shall at once be there.
If from beyond the rolling of the seas
I hear that your neighbours threaten you with terror,
As hostile souls have threatened you before,
I shall come to you with a thousand warriors,
Retainers to help you. I am persuaded that Hygelac,   1830
Lord of the Geats and guardian of his people,
Though he may be young, will be willing to back me
In speech and in service, so that I may rightly
Honour you and bring war-spears to aid you,
The support of our strength, wherever you need men.
If therefore Hrethric your royal son
Should think of the Geatish court, he may find
Many a friend there; he who is himself
Worthy, is the one to seek far shores.'
   Hrothgar in answer spoke to him then: 1840
'These words of yours the Lord in his wisdom
Has sent into your heart; I have heard no man
Utter more reason from a life so young.
You are masterly in strength and sure of mind,
Sense is in your speaking. I do not doubt,
If fate should demand that war in its ruthlessness,
If the spear should take the son of Hrethel,
If sickness or sword-blade should seize your prince
The guardian of his people, and you are still living,

That the Geats over the sea could make no finer   1850
Choice for their kingship, for the keeper of the treasures
Of all the heroes, should it be your consent
To rule in your homeland. Your spirit I cherish
As I grow into its knowledge, beloved Beowulf.
You have brought it about that between these peoples,
The nation of the Danes and the nation of the Geats,
Peace shall pass, and strife shall have truce –
The hostilities and maliciousness they suffered before,
And treasures shall pass as long as I have power
In this spacious kingdom, and many a man   1860
Greet man with gifts where the gannets plunge;
The spiral-prowed ship shall skim the main
With offerings and tokens of our love. I can see
These peoples made steadfast towards ally and enemy,
In everything ingenuous as in days of old.'
     Then the son of Healfdene, protector of men,
Presented him in the hall with a dozen new treasures,
Sending him with these gifts to seek in all safety
His home and his folk, speedily to return.
And the prince of the Scyldings, the king renowned   1870
In every excellence took the best of warriors
By the neck and kissed him; and he shed his tears;
And grey was his head. From the wisdom of his years
He could look for two things, but one was more certain,
That never again would they see one another
As heroes met together. The man was so dear to him
That he could not stem the surging in his breast;
But locked in his heart by the mind's bonds
His hidden longing for the beloved man
Burned on through his blood. Beowulf from him then   1880
Moved out into the field, a warrior fair in gold
Heart-gladdened with treasure. Riding at anchor
The wave-skimmer waited for its owner and lord.
And while they were walking, the liberality of Hrothgar
Was repeatedly extolled; that was one king
To be reproached in nothing – till all joy and force
Fled in him from age which has crushed so many hosts.

The young warrior-band, men brave in fame
Arrived then at the water; they wore their ring-woven
Interlocked mail-coats. The coastguard perceived   1890
The fighters departing as he had seen them come.
He saluted the strangers, and not with insult,
From the head of the cliff; he rode up towards them;
He told them they embarked as brilliant-armoured
Soldiers who would be welcome to the folk of the Weders.
Then that boat was loaded on the shore,
The ring-prowed ship with garments of war,
With the horses and the jewels; the mast soared up
Over the riches from Hrothgar's hoard.
To the man who had guarded the boat he gave   1900
A gold-banded sword, that he thereafter
Could shine at mead-bench the more distinguished
By that treasure, that heirloom. The ship moved off
Swirling through the main, left Denmark behind.
Then to the mast a sea-robe, a sail
Was rope-rigged securely; ship-timber shuddered;
Wave-scudding wind gave there no hindering
To the flood-buoyed voyager; it glided forward
A foam-throated seafarer on the ocean's swell,
Its strong prow probing the roaring streams,   1910
Till they were able to see the cliffs of Geatland,
The promontories of home; the vessel drove
Breeze-blown in and grounded on the beach.
Quickly was the harbour-guard ready at the water,
He who for long had searched the horizon
Yearning by that sea for the beloved men;
The broadbreasted boat he made fast on the shore
With its anchor-ropes, lest pounding of breakers
Should thrust and drag the fine ship away.
Then he had the warriors' treasure taken up,   1920
The ornaments, the beaten gold; he had not far to go
From there to the presence of the jewel-generous
Hygelac, Hrethel's son, to the home where he lives,

Himself and his retinue, beside the sea-rampart.
   Magnificent was the building, the hall towering,
The king in his majesty, Hygd very young
The daughter of Haereth, but wise-minded, distinguished,
For the small succession of years she had witnessed
Within castle walls; nor was she ungenerous
Or too niggardly with gifts, with treasured possessions   1930
To the people of the Geats. – That strong folk-queen
Thryth, now: desperately wicked, and by habit!
None of the heroes of the personal retinue
(But her lord and master!) dared the hazard
Of gazing openly with his eyes upon her,
For he saw in store for him fatal fetters
Human-hand-linked, and then soon after,
Once he had been seized, the sharp-patterned sword
Appointed to make his judgement certain,
To show death's face. Unqueenly ways   1940
For a woman to follow, presuming on her beauty,
When a lady's gentleness turns destroyer
Of a loved man's life for pretended outrage!
But Hemming's kinsman checkmated that:
Men at their ale would go on to tell
How she burdened her people with fewer evils,
Less malign dealing, after she had once
Been given, gold-brilliant, to the youthful champion,
To the beloved prince – after she had voyaged
At her father's bidding across the sallow flood   1950
To the hall of Offa; there now she lived
Known for the good gifts made from her throne,
Taking praiseworthy pleasure in created things,
Knit in noble love with a lord of warriors,
With the most excellent of all mankind,
Of the far-spread race, as his fame speaks,
From sea to sea; and Offa, a man
Eager in the spear-assault, was widely honoured
For liberalities as for war-abilities, and guarded with wisdom
The country in his keeping. Eomer was his son   1960
And a help to men, a kinsman of Hemming,
Grandson of Garmund, strong-armed in battles.

The warrior went then, his retinue with him,
Covering the beach-fields along by the sand,
Broad-stretching shoreland. The world-candle shone,
The south-darting sun. They kept on walking,
They hastened forward to where they knew
The protector of men, the killer of Ongentheow,
The young and excellent warrior ruler
Distributed rings in his castle walls.   1970
Beowulf's coming was at once made known
To Hygelac: the protector of fighters, of shieldsmen
Was arriving there alive in the midst of his courts,
Unscathed from the field, making for his house.
Quickly the interior of the hall was cleared
For those foot-travellers at the king's command.

    The survivor of the conflict sat by him then,
Kinsman facing kinsman, and soon he saluted
His liege lord, his friend, in formal utterance,
With forceful words. The daughter of Haereth   1980
Moved with mead-cups through the hall-building,
She was good to the people, she handed to heroes
The fiery goblet. Hygelac began
Courteously to inquire of his companion there
In that hall of halls – curiosity consumed him –
What sort of adventures the Geats had had.

    'How was your voyage, beloved Beowulf,
When you suddenly determined to seek in the distance
A strife beyond the salty breakers,
A battle in Heorot? Ah, did you redeem   1990
For Hrothgar, the prince, the illustrious, any part
Of his widely-known wretchedness? Anxiety for that
Vexed me with throbbings of care; the exploit
And my love of you clashed, I pled with you continually
To make no attempt on that fiendish killer
But to let the Danes themselves determine
The Grendel struggle. To God I give thanks
That my eyes can see you returned unharmed!'

    Beowulf spoke, Ecgtheow's son:
'Hygelac my lord, the record is candid,   2000
The great encounter is in many minds,

What battle-occasion befell me and Grendel
Within that place where he had relentlessly
Persecuted the Danes with miseries, miseries,
With countless cruelties; I completely avenged it,
And there need be no boasting of that twilight agony
By any of the earthly kin of Grendel,
Whichever of the hated race lives longest
In the chains of crime. Immediately I arrived
To greet Hrothgar there in the ring-hall 2010
The illustrious heir of Healfdene appointed me
A seat by his own son, once he had learned
My mind and purpose. The company rejoiced;
Never have I seen under the arch of heaven
Greater happiness of men at their mead
Sitting in hall. How the famous folk-queen
Guardian of their peace would move throughout the room,
Encouraging the young men; to many making gift
Of a precious ring before she sat again!
And then the ale-flagon, brought before the retinue 2020
To the veterans in turn by Hrothgar's daughter
(Whose name I learned from the hall-banqueters
Was Freawaru) as she proffered to the heroes
The studded treasure-cup! In her youth and gold
She is promised to the courteous son of Froda;
The lord of the Scyldings, the keeper of his kingdom
Has given his agreement, and considers it statesmanship
That by means of this lady the end of great blood-feuds
And struggles may be sealed. On a nation's defeat
How common is the rareness with which the thirsty spear 2030
Takes its hour of rest, for all quality in the bride!
– This now may offend the Heathobard prince
And all the aristocracy among that people,
When he walks with the woman into the hall:
Highborn Danes, the retinue entertained,
And flashing on them heirlooms of men of old,
Hard-edged spiral-patterned treasures of the Heathobards –
Theirs while they had power to wield the weapons,
Before they fatally led to the shield-clash
Their dear companions and their own lives! 2040

Then an old spearsman gazing on the hilt-ring
While men are at their beer-drinking will recall it all to mind,
Spear-death of the soldiers: his heart darkens:
And he begins in his unhappiness to probe the spirit
Of a boy, a fighter, with penetrating purpose,
To stir up war-thoughts, uttering these words:
"Your eyes, my friend – can they recognize the sword,
The priceless metal your father carried
When he went mask-helmeted into battle
For his last battle – where the eager Scyldings   2050
The Danes killed him and held the field
Once Withergyld was dead, once the heroes had fallen?
See now the son of one of the slayers,
He enters the hall exulting in these trappings,
He boasts of the slaughter, and he carries the treasure
Which you and no other should properly possess."
– So time and again he reminds him and incites him
With phrases of bitterness, till the day arrives
When this woman's retainer for his father's deeds
Finds blood-drenched sleep, bereft of breath   2060
By the biting sword-blade; and from there the other
Escapes with his life, the land is familiar to him.
Then on both sides the oaths men swore
Lie violated, and soon fierce hates
Are driving through Ingeld, and in the drifts of care
Colder are the affections he shows towards his wife.
Therefore I think little of this Heathobard amity,
I see scant alliance that is Danish security,
Friendship with solidarity.
                              Now let me go on
With the Grendel story, that you, O treasure-giver,   2070
May rest in the truth of what afterwards happened
In heroic grapplingmatch. Once heaven's jewel
Had swept over the fields, the spirit of wrath
Dusk's fiend, frightful, was moved to visit us
Where we untroubled were guarding the hall.
This was the battle-meeting that struck down Hondscio
Death-evil-fated; he harnessed fightingman
Was the first to fall; he good retainer

In the jaws of Grendel encountered his death-dealer,
The beloved man's body its utter devourer.   2080
Yet none the sooner did the crimson-toothed killer
In the vision of crimes intend to abscond
Empty-handed from the hall of gold;
But with that renowned strength made test of me,
Me his fist flew to seize. His gauntlet dangled
Tremendous, marvellous, fixed by strange clasps:
Masterly all its making and adornment –
With skins of a dragon and a demon's sleights.
He would have me in it, guiltless as I was,
The reckless antagonist wanted me there,   2090
One among many; it was not to be,
After I in my anger stood up to face him.
Too long to tell how I gave requital
To the people's persecutor for every wickedness! –
There, O my prince, I made my acts
An honour to your folk. He fled, he escaped,
For a brief space tasted life's joys,
But his right hand he left behind
In Heorot hall, and from there in humiliation
And misery of mind to the lake-floor he fell.   2100
Kingly recompense the Scylding king granted me
For encounter and kill, in beaten gold,
Rare things, prized things, when morning came
And we took our seats at the banquet-place.
There we had storytelling, there we had music;
The old Scylding, time-schooled, told over the past;
Now the hero of battles awoke the harp's sweetness,
Plucked the happy strings; now sang a poem
Heartbreaking and true; and the great-spirited king
Recited after tradition a narrative of marvels;   2110
And then again the warrior in chains of old age
Would begin to bewail his youth and his war-strength –
His breast was vexed within him, while the crowding
Memories came to him from so many winters.
We thus in the hall the whole day long
Took our pleasure, till night once more
Came down upon men. Soon Grendel's mother

Began then to prepare her sorrow's revenge,
Made a journey with grief; Weders' warring, death
Had seized her son. The fiendish woman 2120
Took toll for her child, she boldly destroyed
A man, Aeschere: wise, an old counsellor:
His living days fled from him there.
Nor could the Danes, when morning came,
Give him up as he lay in death
To be consumed by fire, load some pyre
With the beloved man; she carried off the body
In her monstrous embrace beneath the mountain-torrent.
That to Hrothgar was the sharpest of the afflictions
The leader of the folk had for long suffered. 2130
Now the troubled prince implored me by your life
To make good my nobility in the water-tumult,
To venture out my flesh, to grasp glory;
And vowed me my reward. I then discovered
In that surging pool so many have heard of,
The fierce and terrifying guardian of the abyss.
We fought there, hand-to-hand, for a space;
The lake seethed blood, when in that arena
I slashed off the head of Grendel's mother
With my great sword-blade; I took as by a miracle 2140
My life away from the place – my time
Hadn't come; and the son of Healfdene, protector
Of fightingmen, again gave me countless treasures.
    So the national king followed best custom;
I by no means missed those rewards,
The recompense of strength, but Healfdene's son
Offered me treasures to my own desire
Which my hands, O king of men, shall bring you,
Gladly present to you. Still must every favour
Lie in your giving; it is few, it is few 2150
I have close of kin, Hygelac, except you.'
    Then he had brought in the great flag, the boar-flag,
The battle-riding helmet, the silver-grey chain-mail
And the princely war-sword, and made this speech:
'Hrothgar gave this armour to me,
The king in his wisdom, asking expressly

I should speak to you first about its history;
He told me that for long it had been in the hands
Of Heorogar the ruler and man of the Scyldings;
No sooner for that would he give his son,   2160
Spirited Heoroweard, friends though they were,
The coat of mail. Make full use of all!'
The story tells that four bay horses
Were quickly brought in as the trappings had been;
He bestowed them both as a gift upon him,
Horses and treasures – as a kinsman should,
Shunning secret and crafty web-weaving
Of spite for another, the setting of death-traps
For a comrade in arms. To the hardened fighter,
To Hygelac his nephew was strongly loyal,   2170
And each of them strove to give joy to the other.
We are told he presented to Hygd the torque,
The marvellous jewel-work he received from Wealhtheow
Daughter of the prince – and also three horses
Shining-saddled and lithe; after she had taken
That necklace, what brilliance lay royal on her breast!

    The son of Ecgtheow showed thus his valour,
A man famed in battles and in good deeds,
His acts sought glory; wine-flushed hearth-comrades
Took no death from him; nothing barbarous in his heart,   2180
But he guarded, war-bold, with the greatest wisdom
Of the race of man, that liberal favour
Which God had given him. And for long he was scorned! –
When the sons of the Geats saw little in him,
And the lord of the Weders was loath to grant him
Many possessions at the mead-feast-bench;
It was confidently assumed he was lazy, was dull,
A prince of no spirit. Time brought reversal
To the illustrious man of all he had suffered!

    – The protector of men, war-renowned king   2190
Commanded Hrethel's heirloom to be fetched then
Ornate with gold; no better treasure
Giving sword's service did the Geats then possess;
He laid it down on Beowulf's lap,
And gave him the value of seven thousand –

Acres and capital and castle. For the two of them
That country held inherited land,
Home, ancestral earth, he of higher rank
Owning in particular a spacious kingdom.

[2200-3182] *Beowulf and the Dragon*

Afterwards it happened, in days nearer ours   2200
And tumults of war, when Hygelac lay dead
And battle-sword-blades under the shield-thatch
Brought death to Heardred attacked by the Scylfings,
Dangerous warriors, in the midst of his heroes
The nephew of Hereric violently assailed –
It happened then that the far-spread realm
Came in turn into the hands of Beowulf.
For fifty winters he held good rule –
The king was then advanced in the years' wisdom,
Old the land's guardian – , till a creature, a dragon   2210
Began to tyrannize the black hours of night,
One that kept a treasure-hoard, a towering stone burial-mound
On the upland moor, beneath it a path
Unfamiliar to men. That place was entered
By some soul or other who penetrated far in
Towards the pagan hoard; his hand seized a treasure
Shimmering with jewels; the dragon then avenged it,
Since he lying sleeping had suffered deceit
By stealth of a thief; this the people learned,
The neighbouring clan: his anger had begun.   2220
    Not for his own desire, not of his own accord
Did he who sharp-vexed him force the dragon's hoard,
Only in desperate need had some nameless slave
Of the children of men fled strokes and oppression,
Lost house and home, and made his way in there,
A man guilt-conscious. At once *[. . . . .
. . . .] horror seized the stranger;
Nevertheless the wretched [. . . . .
. . . .
. . . .], when that panic gripped him,   2230

58

The jewelled vessel. Many such riches
Lay there age-old in the vaulted earth,
Left since long ago some man unknown,
Revolving things in his mind, had hidden them in that place,
Testament and abundance of a princely race,
Treasures beyond price. All these death swept,
Years gone, away; and one man remained
From the host of the people, the last wanderer there,
A watchman grieving over friends, to augur
For his own life the same: brief use, brief love   2240
Of long-prized wealth. The barrow of the dead
Stood ready on the plain near the breaking sea,
New-made on the headland, built hard of access;
Into its interior the jewel-guardian took
That cherishable mass of the treasures of men,
Of the beaten gold, and uttered these words:
'Now earth hold fast, since heroes have failed to,
The riches of the race! Was it not from you
That good men once won it? Battle-death, evil
Mortal and terrible has taken every man   2250
Of this folk of mine that has left life and time,
That has gazed its last on feast and gladness.
No one I have to be sword-bearer or burnisher
Of the beaten-gold goblet, the dearly-loved drinking-cup:
That chivalry has slipped away. Hard helmet must shed
Its flashing furnishing, its plating of gold;
Burnishers sleep who should sheen the battle-mask;
So too the mail-coat that has met the biting
Of iron war-blades above clashed shields
Crumbles after its wearer; nor can this chain-armour   2260
Follow the fight's commander into far-off regions
At the heroes' side. There is no harp-pleasure
And no happy minstrelsy, there is no good hawk
To swoop through the hall, there is no swift horse
With hoofbeats in the courtyard. Hatred and death
Have driven out on their voyage the hosts of the living!'
So one sad-minded spoke out the misery
He felt for all, moving unconsoled
Restless day and night, till the tidewater of death

Rose touching his heart. The treasury of delight   2270
Was found lying open by that fiend which from of old
Has gone flaming through the gloaming towards mounds of the
    dead,
Dragon-fiend, swooper sleek-skinned by night
In his sheath of fire, a desperate fear
To region and folk. His it is to search
For the ground-held hoard where he guards agelong
The gold of pagans in profitless ward.
    For three hundred years this scourge of the people
Kept watch within the earth over the titan-hewn
House of treasures, till a certain man   2280
Brought rage into his mind; the beaten-gold goblet
He took back to his overlord, begging reconciliation
At his master's hands. So the treasury was exposed,
The ring-hoard plundered, and pardon granted
To the man in his wretchedness; and for the first time
His lord gazed over that old human handiwork.
When the reptile roused himself, fresh strife was born.
He snuffed along the rock (iron-heart!), saw then
The footprint of his enemy, where he had stepped forward
In his unseen prowling too near the dragon's head.   2290
– As the undoomed man who is still upheld
By the grace of God may with ease survive
Banishment and hardship! Anxiously the treasure-guarder
Examined the ground to discover the man
Who had used his sleep for so deliberately vexing him;
He circled and circled in his flames, savage,
All round the outside of the mound; not a soul
There in the wilderness – but he saw war, rejoiced,
Rejoiced to have battle-action; and he would turn within,
Seeking the fine cup in the cave; he quickly   2300
Found that some man had laid his hands
On the gold, on kings' wealth. The guardian of the treasure
Waited impatiently for twilight to fall;
The keeper of the cave then found his rage,
His hateful purpose to have the price in fire
Of the precious drinking-cup. Now departed day
Filled the reptile's desire; he was able no longer

To wait on the wall, but made off blazing
In flame's panoply. Terrible was that beginning
To the people of the country as soon enough it became   2310
To their own treasure-giver a cruel end.
   The visitant began then to belch glowing flakes,
To burn the fair courts; the glare of fire
Struck horror to men; nothing living would escape
If the persecutor flying in the clouds had his will.
The serpent's attack was seen far and wide,
Both at hand and by rumour the enemy's malicework,
How the lawless war-bringer hated and humiliated
The folk of the Geats. He sped back to the hoard,
To his great hidden hall before the light of day.   2320
He had lapped the inhabitants of the land in fire,
In flame, in blaze; he put faith in his cave,
In his war-cunning and his cave-wall: but his trust failed him.
   Beowulf then was quickly told
The truth about the terror, how his own homestead
The best of buildings, the Geats' royal throne
Was dissolving in waves of flame. Heartbreak
It was to the good warrior, greatest of sorrows;
His wisdom suspected that against ancient law
He had sharply roused the wrath of God,   2330
Of the everlasting Lord; within his breast
Such dark thoughts were surging as he had never known.
The fortress of the people, the country's bulwark,
The sea-bound land had been visited and ravaged
By the flames of the firedrake; the warlike king
The prince of the Weders found him his punishment.
Now the lord of men, protector of warriors
Commanded to be made for him a marvellous battleshield
Entirely of iron; he clearly perceived
That wood of the forest, the limewood buckler   2340
Would fail him in fire. The man proved of old
Was pressing to the end of his life in the world,
Of his lease of days, and the serpent with him
For all his ages of guarding the hoard-riches.
The prince, the ring-giver scorned then to attack
The far-winging creature with a troop of men,

With an armed host; fear was absent
For himself in that contest, nor did he rate high
The reptile's war-ability, his force and his fierceness,
Since he often before, hazarding hardship,   2350
Had survived fights, battle-clashes, after he had swept
Hrothgar's hall clear, a man blessed with triumph,
And crushed in his war-grasp the kin of Grendel
Of hated descent.
                    – That was not the least
Of hand-to-hand encounters where Hygelac was killed,
When the king of the Geats, the folk-prince cherished
Quenched the thirst of swords in Friesland,
The son of Hrethel, struck down by war-blade
In flurries of the fight. From there came Beowulf,
He took to the sea, swam by his own strength,   2360
Shouldering alone thirty outfits
Of war-equipment on his way to the water.
The Hetware had no need to exult in that fray
Fought out on foot when they carried forward
Their shields against him; few came back
From meeting that warrior to visit their homes!
Now the son of Ecgtheow, solitary and in misery,
Swam over the waves' acres returning to his people;
There Hygd offered him the realm and its riches,
King's seat and ring-treasures; she did not believe   2370
That her son was capable of guarding the kingdom
Against foreign attacks now that Hygelac was dead.
No sooner for that could the unhappy folk
See the prince persuaded under any conditions
To become the overlord of Heardred, or to accept
The governance of the realm; nevertheless he acted
As guardian and friend to him among the people,
In kindness and help, ruled over the Geats
Until he should grow older. – Exiled men,
Sons of Ohthere, crossed the sea to him;   2380
They had cast off allegiance to the defender of the Scylfings,
To the best of the sea-kings who made gifts of treasure
In the kingdom of Sweden, an illustrious prince.
That was what brought him to the bounds of death;

His own hospitality won him his wound,
Won the son of Hygelac mortal sword-strokes.
And Heardred once dead, the son of Ongentheow
Turned back again to make for his home,
Leaving Beowulf to guard the throne
And rule over the Geats: a king worth the name!   2390
   He remembered to requite the prince's fall
In later days, he made himself the friend
Of Eadgils in his misfortune, furthered the cause
Of Ohthere's son among his people
Beyond the broad waters with weapons and warriors;
That was his vengeance, in freezing and hazardous
Voyages, and the king he thrust from life.
   So the son of Ecgtheow had survived every fight,
Harsh fray, martial deed, till that one day
When his fate was to offer battle to the serpent.   2400
Now the lord of the Geats, incensed with indignation,
Went with eleven companions to set eyes on the dragon;
He had by then found out how the feud began,
Desperate persecution of the folk: he had received
The great priceless cup from his informant's hand.
He made the thirteenth man in that company,
The one who had caused the outbreak of strife,
Bondman of troubled mind – he, the outcast,
Had to lead the way from there into the country.
Unwillingly he went to where he knew   2410
That one hall of earth was, the subterranean cave
At the sea-swell-verge, beside the clash of waves,
Whose vault was filled with jewels and trappings.
Monstrous was the watchman, vigilant the retaliator
Guarding from of old the underground gold-treasures;
It was no quick purchase for any man to make.
   The war-seasoned king sat down then at the headland;
There the generous lord of the Geats addressed
His hearth-companions. Vexed was his heart
Roving in death's vision, overimminent was fate   2420
That must lay its touch on the aged man,
Track the soul's treasure-hoard, crack and break apart
Body and breath; not long from then

Would the spirit of the prince go wrapped in flesh.
– Beowulf spoke, Ecgtheow's son:
'Many the war-frays, the occasions of battle
I lived through in my youth; how it all comes back to me!
I was seven years old when the master of treasures,
Dear lord of his folk, took me from my father;
Hrethel the king kept me and guarded me,   2430
Gave me feast and gold, never forgot friendship;
Nothing ever made me, as a child at the court,
Stranger to him than any of his sons,
Herebeald or Haethcyn or my own dear Hygelac.
The eldest brother's sudden death-bed
Was spread disastrously by a kinsman's actions,
When Haethcyn struck him, his friend and his lord,
With an arrow drawn from his horn-curved bow,
Shot wide of the target, shot death to his kinsman,
One brother to another by that bolt of blood.   2440
– Combat unatonable, conduct bitterly awry,
A breast-oppressive thought; but the prince nevertheless
Had to leave his life unavenged in its loss.
– Such is the affliction, such is the endurance
Of the grey-haired man whose own young son
Twists on the gallows; then may he keen
In a song of pain, when his boy is hanged
For the raven's joy, and his years and wisdom
Are void of power to bring him any aid.
Morning after morning he is forever recalling   2450
His son in the far marches; he has no anxiety
To live on in longing for another inheritor
Within these courts, where one has met
Destiny's blows in embattled death.
Anguished he scans in his son's dwelling
Desolate wine-hall and wind-vexed resting-place
Wasted of gladness; heroes and horsemen
Sleep in the darkness; no harp sings there
Or happiness to those walls, as they resounded once.
He goes then to his couch; solitary is his elegy   2460
Sung for the solitary: all his castle and country
To him too empty.

       – So the Weders' defender
Laboured under seething sorrowfulness of heart
On Herebeald's account; he had no possibility
Of visiting the killing on the head of the killer;
He could none the more readily harry the warrior
With acts of hatred for his little love of him.
Then in mid-grief which fell on him too sharp
He left human joy, greeted the light of God;
To his sons he bequeathed, as a man who has prospered,   2470
His country and his townships at his life's end.
  Then all was enmity between Swedes and Geats,
Warfare and wickedness across the great waterway,
Relentless fighting once Hrethel was dead
And Ongentheow's sons showed themselves eager,
Not backward in battle, refusing to keep
Friends over the sea, and many times causing
Carnage near Hreosnabeorh, cruelty and horror.
That was avenged, feud and felony,
As fame related, by my kin and friends,   2480
Though one of them paid for it with his own life,
A hard-driven price: the fight finished
Fatal to Haethcyn prince of the Geats.
I believe next morning the other kinsman
Laid punishment on the slayer at the sword's edge,
When Ongentheow was attacking Eofor:
The war-helmet shattered, the old Scylfing fell
Sword-drained of blood, the hand had in memory
Many an encounter and struck unloath to death.
  For the treasures he gave me I paid him again   2490
In time of war, as fate would allow me,
With my flashing sword; he granted me land,
Happy earth and home. There was no need for him
To have to make search in the kingdom of Sweden
Or among the folk of the Danes or the Gifthas
For a warrior who might be weaker, to win him with treasure;
It was always my pride to go before him in the troop,
Alone in the vanguard, and I forever will
Meet the struggle so, while this sword holds
Which has many times served me early and late   2500

Since with these hands, in sight of the retinue,
I killed Daeghrefn, champion of the Franks:
By no means could he bring the king of the Frisians
Those precious jewels, that breast-adornment,
But the bearer of the banner fell in battle,
The prince in his valour; nor did sword kill him,
But a war-clutch crushed his bodily frame
And the floods of his heart. Now edge of blade,
Hand and hard sword must fight for the hoard.'

    Beowulf spoke, uttered his vows   2510
For the last time: 'Many are the battles
I dared when I was young; yet old as I am,
And guardian of this folk, I shall still join fight,
Still deal with glory if that fiend of wickedness
Comes out to attack me from his hall of earth.'
Then he addressed every one of his men,
Vigorous warriors and his dear companions,
On this last occasion: 'I would take no sword,
No weapon to the serpent, if I knew how else
I might come to grips manfully with the monstrous creature   2520
As I did with Grendel in former days;
But I expect to find there blazing fire-enmity,
Breath-fumes, venom; and so I have with me
Chain-mail and shield. I shall not retreat a step
From the watcher of the mound, but from that time on
It shall go with us by the rock as fate ordains for us,
Master of every man. My mind is steadfast;
I may forgo all vaunt against the fighter of the air.
Wait, men, on the mound, with your armour upon you,
Your mail-coats protecting you, for whichever of us two   2530
May be better able to survive the wounding
In our rush to destroy. It is not your destiny,
Not any man's portion unless mine alone
To manifest power in the face of the monster,
To make proof of nobility. I by valour
Shall win the gold, or else war's ill
Mortal and terrible shall take your king!'

    On his shield he rose then, he great warrior
Helmeted and ironminded, went with his battle-mail

Beneath the hanging rocks; his faith was in the strength　　2540
Of one man alone: hardly the category
Of coward's undertaking! He then who had borne
Battles innumerable and clamours of arms,
Man of every excellence where troops should clash,
Saw beside the wall a stone vault set
And a stream there breaking from the burial-barrow;
The boiling watercourse with killing flames
Prevented his staying any time unscorched
In the corridor near the hoard by the dragon's fire.
Then with his rage roused the man of the Geats　　2550
Let speech fly abroad from his throat, the dauntless
Man gave a shout; his loud call of war
Came thundering in under the hoary rock.
Hostility was touched off, the treasure-guardian had heard
The voice of man; the place had seen its last
Moment for peace-suing. First there issued
Out of the stone the breath of the fiend,
Hot fume of fight; the ground resounded.
The warrior in the cave, the lord of the Geats
Swung round his shield to face the strange terror;　　2560
Then the twisted creature found his heart urged
To plunge into combat. The good warrior king
Had his sword drawn, the ancient heirloom
Unslothful of edge; each of them, intent
On the dealing of death, was a horror to the other.
Undaunted the prince of retainers stood up
By his clifflike buckler when the serpent gathered himself
Quickly in his coils; he waited in his armour.
Gliding then he came in his burning folds
Hastening to meet fate. The shield's good defence　　2570
Of body and breath was more short-lived
For the illustrious prince than his desire looked for;
That time and place saw the first day
When he had to do without destiny's decreeing him
Victory in the fight. The lord of the Geats
Swung up his hand and with his ancient heirloom
Struck at the glistening horror, but his blade
Flashing at the bone fell feeble, its bite

Less keen than what was needed by the great-realmed king
In the importuning of his cares. Now after that warstroke   2580
The watcher of the mound grew savage-minded,
Thrust forth his death-fire; far and wide
The war-flashes leapt up. For the Geat gold-giver
There was no vaunting in glorious victories;
His bared battle-blade failed him in the fight
As it never should have done, iron proved of old.
– Uncongenial journey when the great son of Ecgtheow
Was to slip from his hold of that earthly field!
Unwilling he had to find home and rest
In an alien place, as must all men   2590
At close of time's lease.
                           Not much after this
The warrior and the monster came together again.
The hoard-guardian roused himself, his breast once more
Shuddered to his breathing; the old folk-ruler
Fenced round with fire suffered keen distress.
Not one stood by him, of the children of men,
Of his band of comrades, with battle-efforts
And acts of valour, but they fled into the forest
And looked after their lives. The mind of one of them   2600
Was moved with anxieties; nothing can ever
Dissolve kin's duty in right-thinking soul.
  His name was Wiglaf, he was Weohstan's son,
A treasured shieldsman, a Scylding man
And relative of Aelfhere. His liege lord he saw,
His war-masked face in the pain and heat;
He remembered then the land-gift he had once made him,
The prosperous homestead of the Waegmundings,
Every part of the estate, as his father had held;
He could no longer refuse: hand seized shield,
Seized yellow lindenwood, drew ancient sword.   2610
– That heirloom was left among men by Eanmund
Ohthere's son, adventurer, unfriended,
Whom Weohstan was fated to slaughter in fight
At the blade's edge, taking off to his kinsmen
Gold-shimmering helmet and chain-ringed mail-coat
And giant-forged sword of far-off history;

These Onela returned to him, his own kin's battle-trappings,
Armour ready for war – speaking little of the slaying,
Although he had destroyed his brother's son.
He guarded those arms, the corslet and the sword,   2620
Season after season, till his own boy was able
To prove his nobility like his father before him;
At the end, among the Geats, he gave him the war-gear,
Everything in profusion, when he left this life
Voyaging aged away. – Now was the first time
For the warrior in his youth to fight as the comrade
Of his beloved lord in onslaught of battle.
His mind did not soften, nor did his father's sword
Fail him in the encounter: as the dragon discovered
Once they had met and engaged together.   2630
    Wiglaf spoke, to his companions he uttered
In his words many truths – his heart was vexed – :
'I remember the day, where we sat at the mead,
When we made our vow in the beer-banquet-hall
To that lord of ours who gave us those treasures
That we would repay him the trappings of war,
Hard blades and helmets, if need such as this
Should fall upon him. It was for this reason he chose us
From the host, for this hazard, by his express desire,
Thought us men for great acts, and made me those rich gifts: 2640
He considered us sound and worthy spear-warriors,
Eager helmet-bearers – although our lord,
Guardian of his people, meant to accomplish
This task of courage by himself alone,
Since he among men has accomplished the most
In the glories of fame and audacity's actions.
Now that day has come when our liege lord needs
Strength of arms, good fighters; let us go forward,
And give help to our war-leader, in the time of fire,
In this fierce blaze of terror! As for me, God knows   2650
I would infinitely prefer that conflagration
To embrace my body beside my gold-lord.
Unfitting I see it that we should return
Home with our shields, unless we can first
Lay low the adversary, protect the life

Of the prince of the Weders. Certain is my knowledge
That not his deserts dating from of old
Could allow him alone out of the Geatish host
To suffer sorrow and to fall in fight;
War-corslet and chain-mail, helmet and sword   2660
Shall be ours together.' Then he went through the smother,
Took his helmeted head to the help of his lord,
Spoke briefly: 'All things, beloved Beowulf,
Accomplish in excellence as you have told of your youth
Long gone, that your glory you may keep uncrushed
In your living flesh; single-minded prince,
Keen now in your deeds, with all your strength
You must defend your life; my help shall be yours.'
   After those words the dragon came raging,
The malignant terror-bringer fire-surge-flashing   2670
For a second time on the track of his enemies,
Hated race of men. In the waves of flame
Shield burned to its boss and chain-mail was powerless
To afford protection to the youthful spearsman,
But the young man eagerly went in beneath
His kinsman's buckler when his own had been
Destroyed in the fire-flakes. Then again the war-king
Took thought of great deeds and struck with his battlesword
Exerting all strength, till forced by his violence
It stuck in that head: Naegling shattered,   2680
Beowulf's blade ancient and grey
Failed in the fight. It was not his fate
That edges of iron should keep their power
To help him in war; that hand, men say,
Was strong to excess, dangerous in its thrusting
To each sword, each weapon of unspeakable hardness
Taken by him into battle: he had poor help from that.
   Now for a third time the firedrake in its fierceness,
The persecutor of the people paid heed to hostilities,
Rushed the great warrior when his chance lay open,   2690
Scorching and war-cruel crushed all his neck
With the savagery of his tusks; the stain overran him
Of his own life's blood, the red waves flowed.
   Then as I believe, at the great king's need

The warrior by his side made manifest his courage,
His strength and his boldness, as his nature was.
The head he disregarded, but the brave man's hand
Was burned as he brought relief to his kinsman
When he struck a little lower at that body of spite,
The fighter in his armour, till the sword lay plunged,   2700
Plated with its gold and glancing, and the fire
Began then to subside. And again the king himself
Recovering his senses drew the war-knife
Biting and battle-keen he carried on his mail-coat;
The Weders' protector hacked the dragon in half.
Their enemy they had felled: force had driven out
Life: and the two of them as kinsmen and princes
Had brought him to destruction; such should man be,
Such should be a retainer at the hour of need.
To the king it was the last triumph of his hands   2710
Labouring in this world.
                              And now the wound
Which the earth-beast the dragon had given him began
To swell and inflame; he was not long in finding
That the venom was surging within him in his breast
With an enemy's fury. Then wise-minded
The prince went along by the rock till he found
A place where he could sit; he gazed on the handiwork
Of giants, he saw how the ageless cave-hall
Holds fast with its pillars its stone-spanned shell.
Then the retainer immeasurably good   2720
Took water in his hand and laved his war-stained
Friend and lord and illustrious king
Exhausted by battle, and loosened his helmet.
   Beowulf spoke – through his wound's pain
Came his words, through mortal hurt and misery:
Well he knew he had drained his days,
The pleasure of the earth: now time had fled
With all its hours, near, near was death:
'I to my son should at this moment
Be giving my war-gear, were any such heir   2730
Flesh of my flesh granted by fate
To follow after me. I have ruled this folk

71

For fifty winters, and there wasn't a king
Of any country, not any of those about me,
Who dared with warriors to seek me in attack,
To threaten me with terror. I have been patient in the land
For destinies doomed, kept with care what was mine,
Been a shunner of plotcraft and a seldom swearer
Of unrighteous vows. I from all these things
Ill with death's wounds may draw rejoicing,   2740
Since the Lord of men can spare my condemning
For the killing of kinsmen, when this life of mine
Slides from its body. Now quickly go,
Scan the rich hoard under the hoary rock –
Now, beloved Wiglaf, that the dragon lies dead,
Sleeps on outwounded, of his treasure bereft.
Act now with speed, so that I may see
The wealth of old time, the store of gold,
May truly be gazing on the dazzling jewelwork:
So that I by that treasury may be the more assuaged   2750
Leaving the land and life I have long possessed.'
    When these words were spoken, the son of Weohstan
Went I know in haste to obey his lord
Battle-wound-stricken, to carry his chain-mail
The woven coat of war beneath the roof of the cave.
The young retainer saw then, the victor, the darer,
As he went past the seat, gemstones innumerable,
Gold in its glitter littering the ground,
Marvels on the wall along the lair of the reptile
That swooped in twilight from of old, cups standing,   2760
Vessels of a race long lost, lacking
The burnishing hand, torn bare of adornments;
There helmet on helmet lay in rust and time,
And many a bracelet incredibly enchained.
– No man is safe from easy overpowering
By treasure, buried gold, whoever may hide it! –
He saw also hanging high above the hoard
A gold-brilliant banner woven by skilled fingers,
Handiwork of the rarest; it gave off a gleam
By which he was able to see the floor-space,   2770
To gaze over the jewels. Not a sign was there

Of the serpent, for him the sword had seized.
We are told then that the hoard in the barrow of the dead,
Titan-labour of old, by one man was plundered,
When he burdened his lap with plate and cup
At his heart's pleasure; taking too the banner,
Brightest of ensigns. Bitter had the sword been
Of the well-loved lord – iron was its edge –
To him who had held those treasures as protector
Time out of mind, kept terrible fire   2780
Blazing before the hoard, surging in savagery
Midnight after midnight, till he met his killer.
The messenger was in haste, he was anxious to go back
With his precious gains, and desire worried him
To know whether he in his elated mood
Would find the power-spent king of the Weders
Alive in that spot where he had left him before.
With the treasures he came then to where his lord
The illustrious prince lay in his blood
At the close of life; and again he began   2790
To sprinkle him with water, till speech in its sharpness
Broke out from his throat.
                         Beowulf spoke,
The old man from his sorrow gazed over the gold:
'For these precious things let my words voice thanks
To the King of glory and the Lord of all,
To the everlasting God – for what feasts my sight,
That here I have been able to win for my people
A gift such as this before the day of my death.
Now that with my breath, with my years I have bought
The titan-hoard, still look after the nation   2800
In its need; no longer can I be here.
Tell the men of battle to build up a burial-mound
As a splendour after the pyre at the sea-promontory;
It shall rise as a memorial for the people of my race
Towering high upon Hronesness,
So that seafarers of the future may say
"Beowulf's grave", as their ships are driven
Over the streams of darkness from lands far away.'
The great-spirited king took off from his neck

The golden circlet and gave it to the retainer,   2810
To the young spear-fighter, with gold-blazing helmet,
Jewel-ring and chain-mail, wished him joyous use:
'You are the last hope of this family of ours,
Of Waegmunding men; all my own kindred
Destiny has swept off to their death ordained –
Warriors in their daring: and I must win their end.'
That word was the last the old man uttered
From the thoughts of his heart, before he sought the pyre
The fire-wave-fury; the soul left his breast
Mounting to meet the judgement of the just.   2820
   To the man young in years it was now a time
Terrible in its change, when he saw on the ground
The most loved of men at his life's ending
Pitifully placed. His killer lay near him,
The dreadful cave-dragon deprived of breath,
Cornered and destroyed. The crooked reptile
Could rule no longer over rings and riches,
For him the sharpness of swords had seized,
Hard-hammered battle-blades keen in combat,;
And the far-swooping wings transfixed with wounds   2830
Were crushed to the earth at the side of the treasure-store;
The sky saw nothing of his streaming flight
Through the dead of night, unmanifest was the form
Of the glorier in great goods, for he was felled to the ground
By the warrior leader with the power of his hand.
Rare by all accounts indeed is the man
Who prospered in the world, strong though he might be
And one of audacity in every action,
For rushing on the fumes and venom of that enemy
Or touching and disturbing the jewel-hall with his hands,   2840
If he found its guardian waiting and awake
As host of the cave. Beowulf's death
Was payment for the profusion of princely treasures;
Each of them had come to his latest hour
Borrowed from time.
               It was soon after this
That the battle-shirkers came out from the wood,
Ten men together, cowards and vow-breakers

Who had shrunk from throwing a spear in fight
At the hour of their liege lord's heavy need;
But they came in shame carrying their shields,   2850
Their armour of battle where the old man was lying;
Their eyes were on Wiglaf. He in his weariness,
Foot-soldier, sat by the shoulders of his lord,
Tried water to waken him: vain was his work.
Nothing in all the world, though his yearning impelled him,
Could help him to keep that leader alive,
Nor could he pervert what the Lord approved;
Every man's life must lie under the mastery
Of God's decree, as it still lies today.
Grim condemnation from that young man now   2860
Could he quickly expect who had cast away his courage.
Wiglaf spoke, Weohstan's son,
The man vexed at heart scanned hated friends:
'O what but this could the speaker of truth
Say, that the liege lord who gave you those treasures
Of battle-adornment you stand up in there –
And often it was that he proffered at the ale-board
To men sitting in hall chain-mail and helmet,
A prince to his retainers, things as he might find
Of the most magnificent from both far and near –   2870
That he, I say, had utterly, vexatiously wasted
Those war-forged arms, when fighting became his?
Scant cause had he, the king of his people,
To be proud of his campaigners; yet God granted him,
The Lord of all victories, to be able to avenge himself
By his sword alone, when strength was his need.
It was little support that I could give him
For his life in that conflict; nevertheless I plunged
Beyond my own ability to my kinsman's aid;
Our deadly enemy when my sword struck him   2880
Grew feebler and feebler, and the flaming from his head
Poured out less furiously. Too few defenders
Crowded round the prince when that hour assailed him.
Now the treasures received and the swords presented,
Amity and concord, happiness of homeland
Shall perish from your people: and every man

Of that kith and kin shall go dispossessed
Of his lawful lands, when hero and nobleman
Hear from afar the story of your flight
And inglorious action. Death is worthier   2890
For every warrior than days of dishonour!'
    Then he had the news of the encounter proclaimed
In the fortifications up beyond the cliff-top
Where the band of fighters, shieldbearers, sat
The whole morning long, their minds made ready
To receive that day the beloved man
Or his body in death. The rider to the headland
Was sparing of silence in speaking his report,
And truth was in the words he told to them all:
'Now the giver-of-joy generous to the Weders,   2900
The lord of the Geats lies death-bed-bound,
Quiet in blood's couch: it was the dragon's doing:
And beside him lies his life's antagonist
Knife-stroke-broken – with his sword he was helpless
To make any impression, any wound at all
On that monstrous creature. Wiglaf sits by him,
The young son of Weohstan watches over Beowulf,
Warrior over warrior, living over lifeless,
Keeps heavy-hearted guard at the head
Of both the beloved and the hated dead.   2910
    Now may the peoples prepare to see war,
As soon as the king's killing becomes common knowledge
Among Frank and Frisian. The feud took shape,
Steeling the Franks, when Hygelac arrived,
Voyaging with a fleet, at Frisian territory,
And there the Hetware attacked him in battle,
And their vigour and superior strength had issue
In the fall fated for that man-at-arms
When he died with his troops; no treasures were dealt
By that prince to his retinue. We ever after   2920
Had to bear with the missing of Merovingian benevolence.
    Nor have I any trust in passiveness or pledgefastness
Among the people of Sweden, for it was patently seen
How Ongentheow cut off from life
Haethcyn Hrethel's son, there at Ravenswood,

When Geatish men in their vainglorying
First made attack on Swedish fighters.
Quick was the counterthrust Ohthere's old father,
Feared for his cunning, gave in return
When he struck down the sea-king, set free his wife,   2930
He in his old age and she not young,
Gold-plundered, mother of Onela and Ohthere;
And he continued in pursuit of his mortal enemies
Until they evaded him, escaping into Ravenswood
With pain and difficulty, lacking a leader.
Then with a vast force he surrounded them, the wound-weary,
Those still sword-spared, and the whole night through
Threatened and rethreatened the wretched division
With sorrow, saying that when morning came
He would kill some with sword-edge, some by gallows-beam   2940
To gladden the birds. Yet consolation
Broke on them with dawn, on their troubled minds,
When they heard the thrill of horn and trumpet,
The sound of Hygelac, of the good warrior
Following after his own folk-retinue.
– The path of bloodshed, the fierce human strife
Of the Swedes and the Geats was seen far and wide,
How the peoples incited each other to fighting.
Then the renowned, the aged, the great-griefed warrior
Went with his own men to make for his stronghold,   2950
The noble Ongentheow moved farther off;
He had heard of Hygelac's battle-dauntlessness,
The brilliant man's strategy: doubted his defence,
Doubted his ability to resist the seafarers,
To save his treasury, his women and his children
From the voyaging soldiers: the old man from there
Retreated behind his earthwork. Pursuit was given then
To the folk of Sweden, the flags of Hygelac
Flew forward over the whole fortification
Once the rampart was overrun by the thronging Geats.   2960
And there Ongentheow, the grizzled head,
Was driven and cornered at the swords' points
Till that king of men was forced into the hands
Of Eofor alone. He was struck in wrath

By the blade of Wulf, Wonred's son,
So that under the blow the blood sprang streaming
Out through his hair. Unterrified still,
The aged Scylfing speedily repaid
That savage stroke with savager return
When the famous king moved to face him.   2970
The son of Wonred, though active, was unable
To give the old man a retaliating thrust:
He instead first split the helmet on his head,
Making him sink down stained with his blood,
Fall to the ground; but not yet doomed
He raised himself up again for all his deep wound.
Hygelac's retainer when his brother was felled
Grimly allowed his broadbladed sword
Giant-forged, heirloom-steel, to shatter through its shieldguard
The titan-hammered helmet; and then fell the king   2980
The guardian of his folk, he was mortally struck.
Many then were ready to bind up his kinsman,
To lift him away at the first opportunity
Once they could say the field was theirs.
And now warrior Eofor made plunder of the other,
Stripped off from Ongentheow the iron chain-mail,
The tough hilted sword, and his helmet too;
These arms of the old man he took to Hygelac.
He received the war-trappings and pleasantly promised him
Rewards among the people, and performed as he promised;   2990
The lord of the Geats, the son of Hrethel
Gave on his return home battle-recompense
To Eofor and Wulf with priceless gifts,
Presented to each of them a hundred thousandsworth
In land and interlinked ring-money; no man on earth had cause
To reproach him for making those gifts, since they in action had
        earned them;
Finally to Eofor he gave his own daughter
In the sealing of his favour for the gracing of his home.
– This is the hatred and this is the hostility,
The human war-lust I look for now: 3000
That the people of Sweden will try to attack us
As soon as they receive word of the death

Of that lord of ours who for long guarded
The kingdom and its wealth against its enemies,
Saved the keen Scyldings when their heroes fell,
Guided the folk in grace and excelled that guidance
With his manifest nobilities. Best now is haste,
Let us go and gaze on that illustrious king
Who gave us our jewel-rings, and bring him on his journey
To the funeral fire. It is no lonely tribute   3010
That must melt with the hero, but that host of treasures,
Measureless gold from a grim bartering,
And now at the last the ring-riches bought
With his own life's blood; the burning shall devour them,
The blaze shall cover them, not a warrior wear them
As precious memorials, no woman's beauty
Be set in these glories circling her shoulders,
But the two shall be wanderers, far oftener than once,
Sad on strange soil, cut off from gold-gifts
Now that the war-leader has laid aside laughter,   3020
With play and pleasure. For few shall be the hands
That are spared the grasping of the dawn-cold spear,
The fists that must brandish it; and no harp-melody
Shall waken warriors, but the swarthy raven
Ready above the doomed shall be rich in discourse,
And shall speak to the eagle of his own feast-faring
When he and the wolf became thieves of the dead.'
    Such was how the man, the hero related
Tidings for hating; little was his lying
In either word or happening. The whole company rose;   3030
They went without joy in the shadow of Earnaness,
With breaking tears to gaze on that spectacle.
They saw there lying lifeless on the sand
On his couch of quiet him who had once
Been generous to them with jewels; now the last hour
Had reached the good warrior, when the king was killed,
The lord of the Weders, in strange slaughter.
Stranger was the figure their eyes first saw there,
Stretched out opposite, the detested reptile
Lying there on the ground; the firedrake was flame-racked, 3040
Ghastly, maculate with glitter and horror;

Fifty feet long it was where it lay;
Nights had known it, now in its delight
Mastering the wind, now again swooping
Down towards its den; death then bound it,
It had had its last service from subterranean lairs.
There stood beside it cups and flagons,
Plates lay there with precious swords
Pierced through, rust-eaten, as if they had remained
In the hollow of the world for a thousand years: 3050
A heritage, moreover, unusually impregnable:
The long-bequeathed gold was involved with a spell
So that no living soul could have power to penetrate
The treasure-ring-vault unless God himself,
True victor and king, gave one of his choice –
Man is in his keeping! – the opening of the hoard,
Only whatever person seemed fit to him.
    Now men could see how profitless were the practices
Of the creature that criminally hoarded the jewels
In the bowels of the rock: first the guardian   3060
Killed one scant-companied, and then that attack
Was sharply revenged. How hidden the hour
When the unshrinking soldier marches to the close
Of measured years, when man can no more
Be with his kinsmen in mead-hall and home!
So it was with Beowulf, when he went in search
Of cave-watcher and battle-combat: he himself knew nothing
Of the fate by which his life was to be torn from the world.
This was the curse laid heavily on the treasure
By the illustrious princes who placed it there,   3070
That the soul despoiling that spot should be judged
Sin-stained, should be chained fast in hell, should be shut
In those pagan shades, punished and plagued,
Unless the gaze of his Master's grace
Had had prior power on the gold-keen man.
    Wiglaf spoke, Weohstan's son:
'Many for the sake of one must often
Suffer affliction such as we face now.
How could we influence our beloved prince,
The keeper of the kingdom, by any advice,   3080

Against his attacking the gold's guardian –
To let him lie where he long had lain,
Living in that lair until the end of the world?
He followed high fate; the hoard is flung open,
Gained at hard cost; overharsh was the destiny
That drove the great king forward to that place.
I myself entered there and gazed over everything,
The whole hall's treasures, when a chance was given me,
Chance for that venture dangerously given,
To go under the cave-wall. I gathered up in haste   3090
Heavy in my hands an enormous load
Of riches from the hoard, carried it out
Here to my king. Life was still in him,
He was conscious, thinking; many many things
The old man said sorrowing, and told me to speak to you,
Would have you build up, looking back on his actions
As your lord and friend, that burial-mound towering
On the site of the pyre in magnitude and magnificence
Proper to his life as the noblest of warriors
Far throughout the earth while treasures and fortresses   3100
Were his to enjoy. Now again let us hurry,
Let us make for that vision of thick-crowded gemwork,
Rarities under the rock; I shall be your guide;
Till you see close at hand and examine the abundance
Of rich gold and jewel-rings. Let the bier be got ready,
Quickly prepared when we come from the cave,
And then let us take up our king, let us carry
The beloved man to his lasting home
In the Lord's keeping.'
                              Then the son of Weohstan
The war-renowned hero asked for commands   3110
To be given to many of the men of battle,
Of the owners of homesteads, to bring from the distance
Funeral faggots for the land's leader,
To the good man's side: 'Flame now must feed –
The dark fire prosper – on the first of warriors,
On him who so often bore rain-brunt of iron
When the storm of arrows shot from their strings
Streamed on massed shields, shaft in its element

Urging on arrowhead, feather-clad and keen.'
And now the wise-hearted son of Weohstan   3120
Called out from the throng some retainers of the king,
Seven all together, the best of men,
And the eight of them, the soldiers, moved in beneath
That evil vault; the one who went ahead
Held in his hand a flashing firebrand.
No drawing of lots gave robbers to the hoard
While the men had eyes for any part of it
Kept by that hall and no other keeper,
Strewn in decay; none grudged greatly
Their speedy removal of the priceless treasures   3130
Out into the open; the dragon too, the reptile
They pushed over the promontory, let ocean seize him,
Let the flood of the sea engulf that guardian
Of ornaments and arms. Then the wreathed gold
Was loaded onto a wagon – profusion of all things,
And the hero was taken, the grey-headed warrior
To Hronesness.
                    The people of the Geats
Prepared for him then a pyre upon the earth,
Not paltry, but hung round with helmets and war-shields
And shining chain-mail, as his wish had been;   3140
And the illustrious prince their cherished lord
The men lamenting placed in the midst.
Warriors began then to kindle on the headland
The hugest of fires; black above the burning
The wood-smoke rose, the roaring blaze
Mounting through weeping – wind-clamour becalmed –
Until it had broken down, flaring within the breast,
The house of life. In their misery of mind
They bewailed their sorrow, their slaughtered lord;
So too a woman of the Geats, grief-vexed,   3150
Her hair bound up, lamented aloud
And lamented again *[. . . . .
. . . .
. . . .
. . . .] Smoke glutted the sky.
The men of the Weders made then on the headland

A burial stronghold of great breadth and height,
Visible far and wide to voyagers on the sea,
And with ten days' work they had raised the memorial
Of the war-renowned man, surrounding with a wall   3160
What the flames had left: this the most splendidly
That men who had mastery knew how to provide.
Ring-riches and jewel-brooches they laid in the tomb,
Every such adornment as enemies of old
Had taken away from the treasure-hoard;
The wealth of warriors they gave to the earth,
Gave gold to the ground, where it still remains
As useless to creation as it was long ago.
Then famous fighters rode round the mound,
A dozen all told, of the children of men,   3170
To give voice to their pain, to lament their king,
To utter their elegy, to tell the man's history;
They lauded his bravery, and they praised him chivalrously
For audacious deeds, as should always be –
Man's words should honour his lord and friend,
Love lifted up in the hours of death
When his days of living are led to their end.
The men of the Geats, the sharers of his hearth
Mourned thus aloud for the fall of their lord;
They said he had proved of all kings of the world   3180
The kindest of men and the most humane,
Most gentle to his folk, most vigilant of fame.

GLOSSARY OF PROPER NAMES

(The line-number where the name first occurs is given in brackets after each name.)

ABEL (108), the biblical personage, killed by Cain.

AELFHERE (2604), a kinsman of Wiglaf.

AESCHERE (1323), a veteran Danish counsellor, 'Yrmenlaf's elder brother', old friend and comrade-in-arms of Hrothgar; killed and carried off by Grendel's mother avenging her son's death.

BEANSTAN (524), father of Breca.

BEOWULF (18), not the hero of the poem but a Danish king, son of Scyld and grandfather of Hrothgar.

BEOWULF (343 – first referred to, as 'Hygelac's warrior', 194), the hero of the poem; a prince (later king) of the Geats, son of Ecgtheow, and (through his mother) grandson of Hrethel and nephew of Hygelac; brought up with Hrethel's sons; in his boyhood scorned as unenergetic and unpromising, but in later youth renowned for his tenacity in the swimming-match with Breca; voyages to Heorot to help Hrothgar against Grendel, and destroys Grendel and his mother; returns to the land of the Geats, acts as regent after Hygelac's death for the young prince Heardred, and on Heardred's death becomes king himself; rules the Geats for fifty years, and dies while killing the dragon which has been ravaging his country.

BRECA (506), son of Beanstan; a prince of the Brondings; engages in his youth in a famous swimming-match with Beowulf.

BRONDINGS (521), a tribe ruled by Breca.

BROSINGS (1199), owners of the necklace stolen by Hama from Eormenric; probably to be identified with the Brisings or dwarfs from whom Freyja seized her necklace in the Icelandic Elder Edda.

CAIN (107), the biblical personage, and the legendary ancestor of monstrous and malicious creatures such as Grendel and his mother.

DAEGHREFN (2502), a Frankish warrior, killed by Beowulf at the time of Hygelac's invasion of Frankish territory (the Netherlands) in the early sixth century; apparently the killer of Hygelac.

DANES (2), the people ruled by Hrothgar, inhabiting the southern tip of Sweden as well as what is now Denmark; their capital seat Heorot; the poet also calls them Spear-Danes, Ring-Danes, Bright-Danes, East-Danes, West-Danes, North-Danes, Scyldings, and Ingwine: of the variants, only 'Danes' and 'Scyldings' have been used in this translation.

EADGILS (2393), younger son of Ohthere and brother of Eanmund; a Swedish prince who rebels with his brother against the Swedish king, their uncle Onela, and seeks sanctuary at the Geatish court; later, helped by Beowulf, he invades Sweden, kills Onela, and becomes king.

EANMUND (2611), a Swedish prince, elder son of Ohthere and brother of Eadgils; killed by Weohstan.

EARNANESS (3031), 'the eagles' promontory', a Geatish headland near the spot where Beowulf and Wiglaf fight the dragon.

ECGLAF (499), a Dane, father of Unferth.

ECGTHEOW (263), a Waegmunding Geat, husband of Hrethel's only daughter and father of Beowulf.

ECGWELA (1710), an ancient Danish king.

EOFOR (2486), a Geatish warrior, son of Wonred and brother of Wulf; kills the Swedish king Ongentheow, and is rewarded by Hygelac with the hand of his only daughter.

EOMER (1960), son of the Angle king Offa.

EORMENRIC (1200), king of the East Goths; killed himself about A.D. 375.

FINN (1068), king of the Frisians, son of Folcwalda and husband of the Danish princess Hildeburh; in an obscure clash with Hildeburh's brother Hnaef, he and his men besiege Hnaef's group in a hall and force them to surrender, Hnaef himself being killed and his retainer Hengest coming to terms with Finn; the quarrel flares up again after an uneasy winter has passed, and Hnaef's retinue kill Finn and take Hildeburh back to her own people.

FINNS (581), Old English 'Finnas', but probably the Lapps inhabiting the northern Norwegian coast.

FITELA (879), nephew (and son) of the outlaw Sigemund.

FOLCWALDA (1089), father of Finn.

FRANKS (1210), people inhabiting the Netherlands, invaded by the Geats under Hygelac; also called in the poem (but not in the translation) Hugas.

FREAWARU (2023), daughter of Hrothgar and wife of Ingeld.

FRIESLAND (1126), territory of the Frisians, west, east, and north of the Zuyder Zee.

FRISIANS (1094), people in the Zuyder Zee area; those in the east are described as subjects of Finn, those in the west fight with the Franks against Hygelac.

FRODA (2025), king of the Heathobards and father of Ingeld.

GARMUND (1962), father of Offa.

GEATS (205), people inhabiting Sweden south of the great lakes, later incorporated into the Swedish nation; enemies of the Swedes, friends of the Danes; ruled successively by Hrethel, Haethcyn, Hygelac, Heardred, and Beowulf; also referred to in the poem as War-Geats, Sea-

Geats, Weder–Geats, Weders, and Hrethlings: of which names 'Geats' and 'Weders' are used in the translation.

GIFTHAS (2495), East Germanic tribe living near the mouth of the Vistula.

GRENDEL (102), an anthropoid but homicidal monster of extreme strength and ferocity, descended from Cain; haunts the Heorot area, attacking, terrifying, and devouring the Danes; is killed by Beowulf, who thus accomplishes his mission in the first half of the poem.

GUTHLAF (1148), a Danish warrior fighting in Hnaef's retinue against Finn.

HAERETH (1927), father of Hygelac's wife and queen, Hygd.

HAETHCYN (2434), second son of Hrethel the Geatish king; accidentally kills his elder brother Herebeald; rules for a short period after Hrethel's death; killed by the Swedish king Ongentheow at Ravenswood.

HALF-DANES (1069), tribe allied to the Danes; in the story of Finn, it is to this tribe that Hildeburh, Hoc, and Hnaef belong.

HALGA (61), a Danish prince, younger brother of Hrothgar and father of Hrothulf.

HAMA (1198), warrior of continental Germanic (Gothic) tradition who takes the Brosing necklace from Eormenric.

HEALFDENE (57), Danish king, son of Beowulf-the-Scylding and father of Hrothgar.

HEARDRED (2203), Geatish king, son of Hygelac; killed by the Swedish king Onela; succeeded by Beowulf, who had acted as regent while he was still under age.

HEATHOBARDS (2032), Germanic tribe to which Froda and Ingeld belong; perhaps to be identified with the Langobardi or Lombards; their feud with the Danes is hopefully patched up by Hrothgar when he marries his daughter Freawaru to Ingeld.

HEATHOLAF (460), warrior of the Wylfings, killed by Beowulf s father Ecgtheow.

HELMINGS (620), family or tribe to which Hrothgar's queen Wealhtheow belongs.

HEMMING (1944), a kinsman of Offa and of Eomer.

HENGEST (1083), leader of the Half-Danes after the death of Hnaef.

HEOROGAR (61), Danish king, eldest son of Healfdene and elder brother of Hrothgar.

HEOROT (78), the great royal Danish hall 'Hart', built by Hrothgar at what is now Lejre in Zealand; the scene of Beowulf's encounter with Grendel; traditionally destroyed by fire in the Danish-Heathobard vendetta.

HEOROWEARD (2161), son of Heorogar and nephew of Hrothgar.

HEREBEALD (2434), Geatish prince, eldest son of Hrethel; killed accidentally by his brother Haethcyn.

HEREMOD (901), an early and bad Danish king, contrasted with Beowulf.

HERERIC (2205), (probably) Hygd's brother and Heardred's uncle.

HETWARE (2363), a Frankish tribe living in the Lower Rhine area; Hygelac fights against them when he invades the Franks.

HILDEBURH (1071), a princess of the Half-Danes, daughter of Hoc and wife of the Frisian king Finn.

HNAEF (1069), Hildeburh's brother, and leader of the Half-Danes in the fight against Finn, during which he is killed.

HOC (1076), father of Hildeburh and Hnaef.

HONDSCIO (2076), a Geatish warrior in Beowulf's retinue, devoured by Grendel in Heorot.

HREOSNABEORH (2478), a hill in Geatland; the Swedes under Ohthere and Onela attack the Geats here after Hrethel's death.

HRETHEL (374), Geatish king, father of Hygelac, Herebeald, and Haethcyn; dies of grief after Haethcyn has unintentionally shot Herebeald with an arrow.

HRETHRIC (1189), elder son of Hrothgar.

HRONESNESS (2805), 'the whale's promontory', a headland on the Geatish coast where the dying Beowulf wants his burial-mound to be erected, as a landmark to ships at sea and as the memorial of a king.

HROTHGAR (61), Danish king, son of Healfdene, brother of Heorogar and Halga, husband of Wealhtheow, father of Hrethric, Hrothmund, and Freawaru; distinguished ruler, builder of Heorot; friend, counsellor, debtor in service, rewarder, and quasi-father of Beowulf, who by destroying Grendel and Grendel's mother restores the perilous tranquillity of his realm.

HROTHMUND (1189), younger son of Hrothgar.

HROTHULF (1015), son of Hrothgar's younger brother Halga; in spite of Wealhtheow's hopes, his future treacherous behaviour towards his cousins Hrothmund and Hrethric is hinted at by the poem.

HRUNTING (1457), name of Unferth's sword, which he lends to Beowulf for use in his combat with Grendel's mother.

HUNLAFING (1144), either (i) name of a sword, perhaps Hnaef's, which is taken up by Hengest as an earnest of delayed vengeance on Finn, or (ii) a warrior of the Half-Danes, 'son of Hunlaf' (who was perhaps brother of Guthlaf and Oslaf), urging Hengest to exact vengeance by placing a sword in his lap; the present translation takes the former reading, but the passage is, like many details of the Finn episode, still much disputed.

HYGD (1926), wife and queen of Hygelac, daughter of Haereth, and mother of Heardred.

HYGELAC (195), king of the Geats, husband of Hygd, son of Hrethel, uncle of Beowulf, father of Heardred, brother of Herebeald and Haethcyn; killed during his raid of Frankish territory in the Netherlands.

INGELD (2065), prince of the Heathobards, son of Froda, husband of Freawaru.

JUTES (1072), Old English 'Eotan', probably a people subject to the Frisian king Finn, and probably identifiable with the tribe we know as Jutes.

MEROVINGIAN (2921), i.e. Frankish.

NAEGLING (2680), name of Beowulf's sword, used by him when he fights the dragon.

NORWAY (519 – 'on a Norway beach'), literally, 'to the Heathoreamas', a tribe situated in southern Norway, not far from modern Oslo; Beowulf is thrown on this coast after his swimming-match with Breca.

OFFA (1951), king of the continental Angles, husband of Thryth.

OHTHERE (2380), Swedish prince, son of Ongentheow, brother of Onela, father of Eanmund and Eadgils.

ONELA (62), Swedish king, son of Ongentheow, brother of Ohthere; invader of Geatland and killer of Heardred; killed in the counter-invasion of Sweden organized by Beowulf and Eadgils.

ONGENTHEOW (1968), Swedish king, father of Onela and Ohthere; after the capture of his wife by the invading Geatish king Haethcyn, he invades Geatland and kills Haethcyn, but is attacked by Geats under Hygelac near Ravenswood and is killed there by Eofor.

OSLAF (1148), a Danish warrior fighting in Hnaef's retinue against Finn.

RAVENSWOOD (2925), Old English 'Hrefnesholt' or 'Hrefnawudu', a forest in Sweden; here, in the Geat-Swede conflict, Ongentheow kills Haethcyn and is killed by Eofor.

SCANDINAVIA (19), Old English 'Scedeland' or 'Scedenig', the southern tip of the Scandinavian peninsula, at that time a part of Danish territory; used, at line 1686, as an equivalent for 'Denmark', and so translated.

SCYLD SCEFING (4), mythical king, founder of the Scylding (Danish) dynasty; his name may indicate that he was the son of Scef (or Sceaf), but more probably that he was 'the child of the sheaf' and originally an agriculture or fertility figure; moving in the limbo between genealogy and mythology, he has been brought into history to serve the poet's purposes, but the account of his remote and mysteriously patterned life (so reminiscent of Shakespeare's last plays) gains power from its being nearer myth than fact.

SCYLDINGS (30), the Danes in general, or more particularly the reigning Danish dynasty, 'sons of Scyld'; other variants found in the poem, but not translated here, are Honour-Scyldings, Army-Scyldings, and Victory-Scyldings.

SCYLFINGS (2203), the Swedes in general, or more particularly the reigning Swedish dynasty; also called War-Scylfings and Battle-Scylfings.

SIGEMUND (875), son of Waels and uncle (and father) of Fitela.

SWEDES (63), inhabitants of the east central part of what is now Sweden, north of the Geatish territory and the great lakes; traditional enemies of both Geats and Danes.

SWEDEN (2383), that part of present-day Sweden described in the preceding entry.

SWERTING (1203), Hygelac's grandfather or perhaps uncle.

THRYTH (1932), wife of the Angle king Offa; a shrew who has to be (and is) tamed, she serves as contrast to Hygelac's young queen Hygd.

UNFERTH (499), son of Ecglaf and 'thyle' or spokesman of Hrothgar; he 'sits at the feet' of Hrothgar and is a man of importance at the Danish court, combining something of the duties of poet, entertainer, historian, orator, satirist, and general counsellor: being rather like what we should imagine the serious-minded Anglo-Saxons would make of the idea of 'court jester'; he is an egotist, an intellectual, an unpunished fratricide, a privileged and a jealous person, but the *Beowulf* poet with his usual humaneness has given him qualities of military bravery and underlying generosity, and it would be too simple to call him a villain.

WAEGMUNDINGS (2607),family to which Weohstan, Wiglaf, and Beowulf belong; having apparently a Geatish branch (Beowulf and his father Ecgtheow) and a Swedish branch (Weohstan and Wiglaf), in spite of the customary enmity between Swedes and Geats; but perhaps being in reality only Geats, some of whom (e.g. Weohstan) had evidently fought in Swedish service.

WAELS (897), father of Sigemund.

WAYLAND (455), 'the smith' of Germanic legend; Beowulf's coat of mail is his handiwork.

WEALHTHEOW (613), 'a woman of the Helmings', Hrothgar's wife and queen, mother of Hrothmund and Hrethric; her excellence, like that of Hygd, is clearly indicated by the poet.

WEDERS (225), the Geats.

WENDELS (348), a tribe (of which Wulfgar is a chief) not positively identified, perhaps the Vandals, but more likely the inhabitants of either Vendel in Sweden or Vendill in North Jutland.

WEOHSTAN (2602), father of Wiglaf; killer of Eanmund.

WIGLAF (2602), son of Weohstan, of the family of Waegmundings; kinsman of Beowulf; the ideal comrade-in-arms, who alone out of a chosen band of men is willing to risk his life in helping Beowulf to overcome the dragon; to the dying Beowulf Wiglaf is at once the friend in whom pure and naked trust can be placed, the soldier who is an exemplar of honour and selflessness, and the son he never had.

WITHERGYLD (2052), a Heathobard warrior.

WONRED (2971), a Geat, father of Eofor and Wulf.

WULF (2965), a Geat, son of Wonred and brother of Eofor; saved by Eofor when attacked by Ongentheow during the Swedish wars.

WULFGAR (348), a Wendel chief and an official at the Danish court; he introduces the visiting Geats to Hrothgar.

WYLFINGS (461), a Germanic tribe (to which Heatholaf belonged), living perhaps between the Elbe and the Vistula.

YRMENLAF (1324), a Dane, younger brother of Aeschere.